Women Artists

Elke Linda Buchholz

Women Artists

Prestel

Munich • Berlin • London • New York

Contents

The Twentieth Century before 1945

The Twentieth Century after 1945

The Sixteenth Century

Catharina van Hemessen

Sofonisba Anguissola

Barbara Longhi

Lavinia Fontana

Women artists have existed for as long as art itself, but until the sixteenth century their contribution to the history of art remained largely invisible. In the Middle Ages, for instance, artists, both men and women, were rarely mentioned by name. They saw themselves as craftsmen, seldom signed their work and were often active in large workshops, such as those attached to cathedrals. On the other hand, women are invariably included among surviving records of named artists (e.g., lists of guild members), whether as manuscript illuminators, book illustrators or embroiderers. Most women worked in textiles, a highly esteemed art form at the time. The visual arts were dominated by men, however, and such women were always in a minority. Thus, of two thousand medieval manuscript illuminators known by name only about twenty are women.

A new concept of the artist took hold in the course of the fifteenth century, beginning in Italy. The painters and sculptors of the Renaissance recognized that their activity had an intellectual dimension and viewed it in terms of creative originality. These artists proudly signed their work, and some of them, such as Albrecht Dürer, produced self-portraits that expressed this new-found confidence. And whereas the art of the Middle Ages had been concerned chiefly with the world hereafter, Renaissance art focused on human beings and their surroundings. Realistically painted landscapes and interiors depicted with the aid of perspective replaced the monochrome gold grounds characteristic of medieval painting. Even the Virgin Mary appeared not as the aloof Queen of Heaven, but as a beautiful young woman of flesh and blood. Artists now modelled their work on the art of Classical Antiquity, on its ideals of beauty and harmony.

The Italian Renaissance reached its peak around 1500, years when Leonardo da Vinci, Raphael and Michelangelo were working in Florence and Rome and when municipal governments and such noble families as the Medici, the Gonzaga and the d'Este vied with each other to secure the services of the finest artists, thinkers and writers. Flourishing trade and crafts helped create a fertile artistic climate by providing towns and burghers with increased wealth and confidence. Many artists and scholars, including Giorgio Vasari, who chronicled the lives of the most famous artists of his time, were convinced that they were living in an age of cultural achievement unparalleled since Antiquity.

above left
Pieter Bruegel
The Tower of Babel, 1563
Oil on canvas, 114 x 155 cm
Kunsthistorisches Museum,
Vienna

above centre
Albrecht Dürer
Self-portrait, 1500
Oil on panel, 67 x 49 cm
Alte Pinakothek, Munich

above right
Titian
Venus of Urbino, 1538
Oil on canvas, 119.5 x 165 cm
Galleria degli Uffizi,
Florence

Raphael
Madonna del Belvedere,
1505/06
Oil on panel, 113 x 88.5 cm
Kunsthistorisches Museum,
Vienna

In the course of his career Michelangelo gradually departed from the harmonious ideals of the Renaissance. The art of the era he ushered in is called Mannerism. This was a period of great stylistic variety and experiment, of daring compositions, stark contrasts and bold effects. New parameters for religious imagery, which continued to dominate the visual arts, were established in the sixteenth century by the Catholic Church at the Council of Trent. The Council was convened in response to the upheavals brought about by Martin Luther and the Reformation, which had shaken the foundations of the Christian faith and Church in northern Europe. The Catholic Counter-Reformation strengthened the position of the Pope and promoted veneration of the Virgin Mary and the saints. According to Counter-Reformation tenets, Christian art should be didactic and therefore easily intelligible, encouraging the faithful to 'imitate the saints in their life and morals and to worship and love God'.

For women the Counter-Reformation meant a step backwards. More than before, they were restricted to playing a role in the Christian family, as virtuous virgins, faithful wives and caring mothers. In the Renaissance at least the status of upper-class women had improved, with such intelligent, cultivated figures as the poet Vittoria Colonna and the patron of the arts Isabella d'Este known and respected beyond the borders of their native country. Nevertheless, women were rarely able to acquire professional training and pursue independent careers in commerce or the arts and crafts. Painting was no exception, yet here and there women artists emerged from obscurity and survive as distinct personalities. Some forty women artists are known to us from sixteenth-century Italy. Only a handful of them achieved more than local recognition and almost without exception they were the daughters of painters, who had grown up in artistic surroundings. It is frequently impossible to ascertain the share of such women in the production of their fathers' workshops, since unsigned work is difficult to ascribe to specific workshop members.

A few women artists, such as Sofonisba Anguissola and Lavinia Fontana, did achieve success and fame in the Renaissance, though they were subsequently forgotten. Contemporaries regarded them as 'miracles of nature' and lauded them as exceptional cases. After all, they gave the lie to the conventional view that women possessed no creative ability. These renowned women painters became inspirational models for subsequent generations. Thus, the sixteenth century saw the establishment of a specifically female tradition in the fine arts.

Women Artists in Convents

In the Middle Ages monasteries were important centres of cultural and intellectual life in Europe. They were places of prayer and meditation, reading and writing, painting and composing, and places in which Greek and Latin were taught. Until the sixteenth century convents frequently offered the only opportunities for women to indulge in intellectual and artistic pursuits. They had to pay a price for this, leading a life of complete seclusion in accordance with strict rules and taking an oath to preserve their virginity. Women did not always become nuns of their own free will. Often noblemen and burghers gave their daughters into the custody of a convent rather than pay a dowry.

Artistically gifted women were welcome in convents. Many nuns spent their entire lives in the convent scriptorium copying and illustrating the Holy Scriptures and other devotional texts. By decorating the pages of the manuscripts with precious borders, gold letters and colourful pictures, they were praising the word of God. Occasionally, they would proudly attest to their achievement by including an image of themselves in a richly ornamented initial. The twelfth-century nun Guda did this, and so did Maria Ormani in a manuscript she illustrated three centuries later in Florence. Caterina de Vigri, a member of the convent of the Poor Clares in Bologna in the fifteenth century,

Andriola de Barrachis, *Madonna and Child,* 1485
Oil on panel, 100 x 50 cm, Monastero di Santa Felice,
Pinacoteca Malaspina, Pavia

achieved great renown, although not because she created book illustrations, frescoes and panel paintings, but because she was venerated as St Catherine of Bologna. For her and other artist-nuns, penetrating the meaning of the Scriptures

was far more important than displays of artistic skill.

Nuns did not restrict their artistic activity to illustrating codices. At the Cistercian monastery of Wienhausen in Germany, for instance, they took up brush and paint in the fifteenth century to decorate the choir of their church, while at Pavia in Italy in 1489 Andriola de Baracchis, abbess of the local convent, signed an altar painting of the Virgin Mary holding the Christ Child, his hand raised in blessing, with a group of nuns in their monastic robes at her feet. In Florence the influential Dominican preacher Girolamo Savonarola encouraged nuns in his order to engage in artistic activity. The best known of them was the abbess Plautilla Nelli (1523–1588), who entered a convent at the age of fourteen and subsequently taught painting to her fellow nuns. Giorgio Vasari, the contemporary chronicler of Italian art, reports that, although Nelli had next to no contact with the world of art outside her convent, her images of the Madonna were so greatly admired that private patrons in Florence commissioned examples from her.

During the Renaissance monasteries became less important artistically, as printing with movable type spread and secular subjects gained in significance. Although nuns continued to paint in later centuries, the finest women artists were no longer to be found in convents.

Events in History: The Sixteenth Century

1421
Giovanni di Bicci de' Medici is elected *Gonfaloniere* of Florence, becoming the founder of the Medici dynasty.

1450
In Mainz, Johannes Gutenberg invents the printing press with movable type.

1485
Leon Battista Alberti's seminal work

De re aedificatoria is the first book on architecture to be printed.

1492
Christopher Columbus discovers America.

***c.* 1503-06**
Leonardo da Vinci paints the *Mona Lisa*.

1517
Martin Luther nails his ninety-five

theses to the door of the castle church in Wittenberg.

1550
Giorgio Vasari publishes his *Lives of the Artists*, which lays the foundation for later study of art history in the West.

1569
Gerardus Mercator produces his world map for seafarers.

1590
The dome of St Peter's in Rome is completed according to plans by Michelangelo (based on designs by Donato Bramante).

1600
William Shakespeare starts work on *Hamlet*, the first of his great tragedies.

Catharina van Hemessen

In the sixteenth century Antwerp was a flourishing commercial and artistic centre that afforded many artists a living. It was here that Pieter Aertsen created his bustling market pictures, that artists who had trained in Italy, such as Frans Floris, introduced Renaissance ideas to the art of their native country and that Pieter Brueghel the Elder painted his famous images of proverbs and peasants. Catharina van Hemessen, the earliest Flemish woman artist whose work is still well known, belonged to this generation.

Van Hemessen's father, Jan, was a successful painter of altarpieces and Classical allegories. Having trained his daughter as an artist, he enlisted her aid in carrying out commissions. Family members often helped out in an artist's workshop, but usually anonymously because sons and daughters were not required to register with the local painters' guild. Catharina van Hemessen, however, painted pictures of her own and made sure her name was not forgotten: 'Catharina de Hemessen pingebat 1551' (Catharina van Hemessen painted this in 1551), for example, appears in bold white letters on her *Portrait of a Lady* in the National Gallery, London.

This is an official portrait. The subject appears dignified and aloof, conscious of her social standing. Such details as the transparent lace headgear and the curled hair are rendered with the greatest precision. Small dogs of the kind held by the woman were popular among elegant ladies and a symbol of faithfulness. Van Hemessen has used light and shade to model the young woman's striking features softly; the hint of a smile plays across her lips. The plain background must have made the portrait seem rather old-fashioned to contemporaries, but the woman's personality is conveyed vividly. Like many of Van Hemessen's works, the picture is small compared with those painted by her father. Painted on wood panel, this and other carefully executed portraits by her possess something of the charm of miniatures. Three years earlier, at the age of twenty, Van Hemessen had painted a self-portrait that shows her at the easel with brush, palette and mahlstick. This is one of the first self-portraits in which an artist depicted him- or herself at work.

The young painter came to the notice of Mary of Hungary, regent of the Netherlands and sister to Charles V, Holy Roman Emperor and King of Spain. 'Little Catharina' is documented in 1555 as a member of the court of this intelligent and cultivated ruler, an important patron of the arts who had her portrait painted by no less an artist than Titian. Van Hemessen and her husband, the Antwerp composer and organist Chrétien de Morien, accompanied Mary when she returned to Spain in 1556. After this date no work by her has survived. Indeed, no more than ten signed paintings by Van Hemessen are known, the majority of them portraits, the others religious images.

Catharina van Hemessen
b. 1528 Antwerp
d. c. 1565

- *trained under her father, Jan van Hemessen*
- *surviving works: about ten signed paintings (1548–55) and others attributed to her*
- *see her work, for example, in the National Gallery, London, the Wallraf-Richartz-Museum, Cologne, the Rijksmuseum, Amsterdam, and the Musée des Beaux-Arts, Brussels*

Catharina van Hemessen
Portrait of a Lady, 1551
Oil on panel, 23 x 18 cm
National Gallery, London

CATHARINA DE
HEMESSEN
PINGEBAT
1551

Sofonisba Anguissola

Sofonisba Anguissola and her sisters represent a great exception in sixteenth-century art. At a time when artistic activity of any kind was very rarely open to women in Italy four out of six sisters in the Anguissola family became painters. Furthermore, their father, Amilcare Anguissola, was not a painter. He was a nobleman of Cremona who had been educated by Humanists and put into practice a demand made by some contemporary authors, including Baldassare Castiglione, that not only the sons, but also the daughters of high-ranking parents should receive an extensive education in literature, music, philosophy and drawing. Anguissola's eldest daughter, Sofonisba, showed such promise that the instruction in drawing she received from Bernardino Campi soon turned into fully fledged training as a painter. Amilcare Anguissola gave his gifted daughter every support, introducing her to influential circles and sending examples of her work to courts throughout Italy.

Giorgio Vasari, the painter and chronicler of Italian art, was most enthusiastic about Sofonisba's paintings when he visited the Anguissola family in Cremona. They were, he wrote, 'so excellently done that one fancies they have breath and life'. Vasari was especially impressed by Sofonisba's picture of her sisters playing chess, which she painted at about the age of twenty. This was an extremely unusual image for Italian painting of the time. Instead of painting a conventional group portrait, Sofonisba chose to depict an everyday scene in which the feelings and personalities of the young girls are given vivid expression. Her hand on a chess piece, Lucia looks at the viewer while little Europa laughs at her sister Minerva's surprised reaction to the latest move in the game. An elderly servant watches from the right. Europa's mischievous laugh is without parallel in the painting of the day and, indeed, contemporaries particularly valued Sofonisba's ability to depict emotions and facial expressions. Her drawings of laughing girls and crying boys were well known in Rome's artistic circles. No less a person than Michelangelo expressed admiration for them and, at her father's request, sent the young artist some of his own drawings for study purposes. Sofonisba's self-portraits were soon to be found in Italy's finest art collections, and over a dozen of them have survived – more than by any other artist of that time.

By 1559 Sofonisba Anguissola had become so famous that King Philip II of Spain called her to Madrid to teach drawing to his young queen, Isabella. In the portraits she painted in Madrid the artist had to adopt the strict conventions governing court portraiture in Spain. For a long time many of these portraits, which she did not sign, were attributed to other court painters.

When Anguissola left the King's service after ten years she was granted a generous pension for life and a marriage was arranged for her with a Sicilian nobleman. He died young, and only then does she seem to have achieved personal happiness. At a quickly organized wedding – a rarity in those days – she married the captain of the ship in which she was returning from Sicily to her native northern Italy. Anguissola remained a well-known figure into her old age, and shortly before her death the Flemish painter Anthony van Dyck visited the eighty-year-old and sketched her portrait.

Sofonisba Anguissola
b. *c.* 1532 Cremona
d. 1625 Palermo

- *trained under Bernardino Campi and Il Sojaro*
- *executed mainly portraits, including many self-portraits*
- *painter to the court of Spain, 1559-73*
- *first Italian woman painter of international repute*

Sofonisba Anguissola
The Artist's Sisters Playing Chess, 1555
Oil on canvas, 72 x 97 cm
Muzeum Norodowe, Poznan

Barbara Longhi

A trace of sadness lies on the soft, idealized features of the Madonna. Her eyelids are lowered, her head tilted gracefully. Held in her lap, the boy Jesus turns affectionately towards the young St John, who holds a reed cross in reference to the fact that he will one day baptize Christ in the waters of the River Jordan. Mary places her arms protectively around the two boys. She knows that Christ will sacrifice himself on the Cross, and the painting encourages the viewer to reflect on this. Everything is redolent of clarity and harmony: the gently curving lines, the soft roundness of the bodies, the colours and the equilateral triangle underlying the composition. Mary and Jesus are set off against a dark curtain, draped behind them as a symbol of their special status. This contrasts with the distant view of a landscape behind St John, its river recalling the Jordan.

This type of image was invented in the fifteenth century. Renaissance artists such as Leonardo da Vinci and Raphael had infused their pictures of the Virgin and Child with an idealized beauty and a harmony based on geometry, and their works became models for generation upon generation of painters, including that of Barbara Longhi. Madonnas were her speciality: twelve of her fifteen surviving works depict the Virgin and Child. Devotional images of this kind were extremely popular as a result of the revival of the cult of the Virgin promoted in the Counter-Reformation.

Evidently, neither the artist nor her patrons were much concerned with stylistic innovation. Longhi spent her entire life in her provincial home town of Ravenna in northern Italy, far removed from the artistic centres of Rome, Florence and Bologna, where the style of the High Renaissance had already given way to Mannerism. Yet Giorgio Vasari, painter and historian of the art of his day, took note of the artist during a visit to Ravenna and, in 1568, included her in the second edition of his biographies of famous artists. She was only sixteen years old at the time. 'Maestro Luca de' Longhi, of Ravenna, has painted many beautiful pictures in oil, with numerous portraits from the life, in his native city and its neighbourhood... Nor will I omit to mention that a daughter of his, called Barbara, still but a little child, draws very well, and has begun to paint also in a very good manner and with much grace.'

We know next to nothing about Longhi's life. Like her elder brother Francesco, she learned the art of painting from her father, Luca, and was subsequently a member of his workshop. Barbara's paintings are difficult to distinguish from those of Luca, but she did at least inscribe some of them with the letters 'BLF', standing for 'Barbara Longhi fecit' (made by Barbara Longhi). Her Madonnas are especially notable for their aura of deep calm. Although her portraits were much admired by contemporaries, very few have survived. Neither do we possess a self-portrait by her. Perhaps, however, she immortalized her features in those of St Catharine or St Barbara, in the way that her male counterparts sometimes depicted themselves in the guise of saints.

Barbara Longhi
b. 1552 Ravenna
d. 1638 Ravenna

- *trained under and collaborated with her father, Luca Longhi*
- *executed mainly religious paintings, especially pictures of the Madonna*
- *see her work, for example, in the Pinacoteca, Ravenna, the Gemäldegalerie, Dresden, and the Walters Art Gallery, Baltimore, Maryland*
- *influenced by Correggio, Leonardo, Raphael and the engravings of Marcantonio Raimondi*

Barbara Longhi
Virgin and Child with the Infant Saint John the Baptist
Oil on canvas, 88.5 x 71 cm
Staatliche Kunstsammlung Dresden, Gemäldegalerie
Alte Meister, Dresden

Lavinia Fontana

Study of the naked human body has formed the basis of all academic artistic training since the Renaissance, yet centuries later it was still viewed as unsuitable for women. Women artists who did not engage in such study secretly might experience difficulty in depicting figures for the rest of their lives. Female nudes painted by women were especially rare, but Lavinia Fontana had a sure command of the genre, as revealed in works commissioned from her by private patrons.

Fontana's Minerva, the Antique goddess of the arts and of war, looks gracefully over her shoulder at the viewer. Having laid aside her weapons, helmet and shield, she is about to don an elegant robe. The figure, which is one of exquisite beauty, exudes an aura of calm and natural ease, her nakedness neither inviting a voyeuristic gaze nor appearing sexually suggestive.

This is the last picture Fontana painted. More than one hundred works by her have survived. They range from small devotional images to ambitious altarpieces, from official portraits to paintings on subjects drawn from Classical mythology. Fontana was the first woman artist to compete successfully with men on the art market without the security afforded by a monastery or by the post of court artist. She achieved international recognition in her own lifetime. In a circular self-portrait, commissioned by a collector for his portrait gallery, Fontana shows herself studying Antique nude statues, thus laying claim to high artistic status.

The artist's father and teacher, Prospero Fontana, was the leading painter in Bologna, a major artistic centre at the time. As chairman of the local painters' guild, he no doubt made it possible for his daughter to practise painting professionally without belonging officially to the guild. She had the added advantage of marrying a wealthy nobleman, Gianpaolo Zappi, himself a trained painter. As an artist,

Zappi was far inferior to his wife and, in a reversal of the customary roles, is thought to have functioned as her assistant, helping with the draperies in her paintings.

In the years following her marriage Fontana gave birth to eleven children (most of whom did not survive childhood), but continued her work as an artist with undiminished energy. Initially, she painted small religious images and made a name for herself as a portraitist among the scholars of Bologna's renowned university. Her lifesize portrait of the family of the influential Bologna senator Gozzadini surpassed in its dimensions alone any image of this type previously produced in her home town. For decades afterwards Fontana made a comfortable living painting expensive portraits of noblewomen.

Fontana was the first woman artist in Italy to create large-scale altar paintings and received commissions of this kind from Rome. She eventually moved there with her family in order to fulfil a commission for a picture larger than any ever executed by a woman – an altarpiece more than six metres high in the basilica of San Paolo fuori le mura. Regrettably, it was destroyed in a fire in the church.

Lavinia Fontana
b. 1552 Bologna
d. 11 August 1614 Rome

- *trained under her father, Prospero Fontana*
- *first woman artist to execute numerous large altarpieces and nudes*
- *over 100 surviving works, the largest body of work of any pre-18th century woman artist*
- *King of Spain paid 1,000 ducats for her 'Holy Family'*

Lavinia Fontana
Minerva Dressing, 1613
Oil on canvas, 260 x 190 cm
Galleria Borghese, Rome

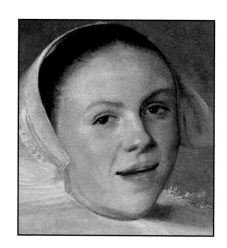

The Seventeenth Century

Artemisia Gentileschi

Clara Peeters

Judith Leyster

Elisabetta Sirani

Maria Sibylla Merian

Rachel Ruysch

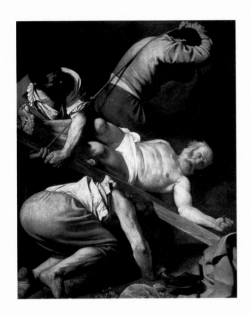

nbrandt Harmenszoon van Rijn   Bartolomé Esteban Murillo   Willem Kalf   Jacob van Ruisdael   Jan Vermeer   Andrea Pozzo   Jean-Antoine Watteau

The seventeenth century was the age of absolutism and religious wars. In France Louis XIV, the 'Sun King', enjoyed limitless power; in Rome the Popes lived in state like royalty; and in Spain the Crown ruled with a rod of Inquisitorial iron. While the southern Netherlands remained under Spanish rule, the Protestant north won independence and, as the republican United Provinces, became a major commercial power. In Germany the Thirty Years' War paralysed the economy and the arts; only in the second half of the century did its rulers promote the visual arts, taking their cue from France. In France, Italy, Spain and the Netherlands the seventeenth century – the Baroque era – was reckoned to be a 'golden age' of art.

Quite different styles were cultivated in the various countries of Europe. Early in the century, in Rome, Caravaggio created a sensation with realistically painted, dramatically lit pictures. This type of image, which was widely imitated, ushered in the Baroque style of painting in Italy. Religious art flourished under the patronage of the Popes, while the gods of Classical Antiquity invaded the palaces of the nobility. Mythological subjects, often embedded in idealized landscapes, also played an important part in the work of French artists, including Nicolas Poussin and Claude Lorrain. Such outstanding painters as Bartolomé Esteban Murillo, Diego Velázquez and Francisco de Zurbarán dominated Spanish art with starkly compelling portraits and images of the saints. In Antwerp Peter Paul Rubens became a celebrated prince among painters. To this day, his monumental altarpieces and history paintings are considered to be the very epitome of the Baroque style. These are rousing images, full of a voluptuous three-dimensionality, that engage the emotions of the viewer through a dynamic visual language characterized by dramatic lighting, bold colours and broad, sweeping strokes of the brush.

While Rubens and his fellow artists in the Spanish Netherlands, among them Anthony van Dyck and Frans Snyders, worked mainly for aristocratic patrons, in the northern Netherlands another type of client set its stamp on the country's art and culture. Most members of the middle classes – not only the wealthiest burghers – felt the need to surround themselves with works of art. As a result, painting flourished to an extraordinary degree: it has been estimated that some 3,200 painters were active in

above left
Michelangelo Merisi da Caravaggio
The Crucifixion of Saint Peter, c. 1600
Oil on canvas, 232 x 201 cm
Cerasi Chapel, Santa Maria del Popolo, Rome

above centre
Peter Paul Rubens
The Rape of the Daughters of Leucippus by Castor and Pollux, 1618
Oil on canvas, 224 x 210.5 cm
Bayerische Staatsgemäldesammlungen, Alte Pinakothek, Munich

above right
Rembrandt
Self-portrait, 1658
Oil on canvas, 133.5 x 104 cm
The Frick Collection, New York

Frans Hals
Malle Babbe, 1633-35
Oil on canvas, 75 x 64 cm
Museen Dahlem, Berlin

the United Provinces in the seventeenth century. Such developments promoted certain types of subject matter: independent still lifes, landscapes and genre pictures (scenes from everyday life) became increasingly popular. Motifs derived from their daily surroundings particularly appealed to the new class of buyer. Many artists became specialists. There were flower and animal painters, artists who devoted themselves to hunting scenes or still life, to winter landscapes or seascapes, to church interiors or tavern scenes, to portraits of middle-class sitters or biblical subjects. The range of styles was equally extensive. The meticulous manner of a Gerrit Dou was as highly valued as the free brushwork of a Frans Hals, the restrained perfection of Jan Vermeer as highly as the bold roughness of Rembrandt. The extreme naturalism with which materials are depicted in Dutch seventeenth-century painting – shiny silk, glittering brass, soft animal hair, delicate flowers and so forth – addresses all the viewer's senses. Realism also won the day in portraiture. Rembrandt was its outstanding exponent. In countless self-portraits he made his own face the subject of artistic reflection.

The profession of artist had long established itself as one with a moral and intellectual dimension. Like tradesmen, however, artists throughout Europe were still organized in guilds. Every large town had a guild for painters, frame-makers and sculptors, usually named after St Luke, who according to legend had painted an image of the Virgin Mary. The guild regulated training, prices and competition. Only members were allowed to practise locally as painters, accept apprentices and offer their work for sale. Women were not generally excluded explicitly from the guilds, but an artist such as Judith Leyster, who maintained a workshop with several apprentices in Haarlem, remained a rarity in the seventeenth century. Over a hundred-year period, for instance, the painters' guild in Delft numbered only two women among its 352 members. Documents refer more frequently to painters' wives, either as having taken over their husband's workshop after his death or managing the sale of his work. Women are, in any case, encountered relatively often in commercial contexts in the United Provinces, and since artists frequently lived and worked on the same premises it was easy for their wives and daughters to participate in workshop activity. These women were generally accorded secondary tasks, such as producing copies of sought-after paintings.

Yet the number of women artists did increase, and examples such as Leyster, Rachel Ruysch and Elisabetta Sirani show that in the fertile artistic climate of the seventeenth century a determined woman could compete successfully with male colleagues on the free market. Almost without exception, the well-known women artists of this time came from two areas of society – from the families of artists or from the educated upper classes. This is scarcely surprising if one remembers that artistic training had to be paid for and that young women were destined for the role of wife and mother.

Artemisia Gentileschi

The killing of Holofernes is depicted in this painting with startling immediacy. The figures appear to have emerged suddenly from the nocturnal gloom. The young Jewish heroine Judith is about to decapitate the bearded Assyrian general while her maid holds down his body on the bed. Her sleeves pushed up above her elbows, Judith summons all her strength in wielding the sword. Determination and physical effort are written in her face. She commits the deed as though performing an unpleasant but necessary duty. Having courageously stolen forth from her people's besieged city to the enemy camp, she plied Holofernes with drink so as to be able to overcome the man who had thought to seduce her.

The Apocryphal story of Judith and Holofernes has always captured the imagination of painters and sculptors, especially in Italy in the sixteenth and seventeenth centuries. Artemisia Gentileschi was certainly familiar with a painting by Caravaggio in which the Roman artist rendered Judith's bloody deed with alarming force. Gentileschi brings the figures even more closely together in the foreground and intensifies the effect of the scene by dramatic lighting. The painting is disturbing not only because of its unvarnished representation of a murder, but also because the perpetrators are women. The picture, the artist's best known, was not her only treatment of the subject.

In Gentileschi's images women are depicted as strong in character, as beautiful heroines with powerful bodies who assert themselves in extreme situations. They are generally famous figures of history or legend, such as Susanna, Cleopatra, Lucretia, Bathsheba, Delilah and Esther. The artist shows them harassed or threatened by men or, as with Judith, triumphing over them.

Gentileschi had experienced male violence at first hand. At the age of eighteen she was raped by one of her teachers, Agostino Tassi, in her father's workshop, where she trained as a painter. Orazio Gentileschi did not take his erstwhile friend to court until one year later, Tassi having attempted to avoid punishment by promising to marry Artemisia – a common 'solution' in such cases. The court case caused a scandal and dragged on for months, making Artemisia's situation still worse. Under torture by thumb screw she was compelled to reveal every detail of the rape and to submit to gynaecological examination. Although Tassi was eventually sentenced to several months' imprisonment, Artemisia's reputation was ruined.

Shortly afterwards Gentileschi married the Florentine painter Pierantonio Stiattesi and moved with him to his native city, where she bore four children in the space of a few years. She soon established herself in Florence as an influential artist, but she later separated from her husband and worked in Rome, Naples and London. As tastes changed over the decades Gentileschi found it increasingly difficult to market her type of stark realism à la Caravaggio, but she was never willing to accept less favourable terms than male artists simply because she was a woman.

Artemisia Gentileschi
b. 8 July 1593 Rome
d. 1652/53 Naples

- *trained under father, Orazio Gentileschi, a pupil of Caravaggio*
- *admitted to the Accademia del Disegno in Florence in 1616*
- *worked alongside her father for Queen Henrietta Maria in London in 1639*
- *important representative of the generation of artists influenced by Caravaggio*

opposite
Artemisia Gentileschi
Judith Beheading Holofernes, c. 1620
Oil on canvas, 169 x 162 cm
Galleria degli Uffizi, Florence

Michelangelo Merisi da Caravaggio
Judith Beheading Holofernes, 1595–96
Oil on canvas, 145 x 195 cm
Galleria Nazionale d'Arte Antica, Palazzo Barberini, Rome

Clara Peeters

For the wealthy burghers of the Netherlands it was a novelty when artists began painting precious vessels, glittering gold, exquisite flowers and rare shells so naturalistically that one felt one could touch them. The artist arranged the sought-after collector's items on a table, the front edge of which she inscribed in the painting 'CLARA P. ANNO 1612' (Clara P. in the year 1612). Clara Peeters belonged among the pioneers of still-life painting. In the Netherlands still life, so called because it depicts inanimate objects, became one of the most popular artistic genres in the course of the seventeenth century.

Half the then-known world is represented in the painting. The gold coins had been minted recently in Spain. Lidded goblets of this kind were made in Germany around 1600, and the shiny white dish is a piece of precious Chinese porcelain, introduced to Europe only eight years previously. The exotic shells, too, would have found a treasured place in contemporary chambers of curiosities. The artist certainly did not own the objects, however often valuable items of this kind appear in her paintings. No doubt they belonged to the wealthy individual who commissioned the picture. In combining expensive arts and crafts items with a plain bunch of flowers, Peeters may have been giving her painting an allegorical dimension. Such *vanitas* still lifes, which were common in the seventeenth century, drew attention to the transience of life and everything else in this world (*vanitas* means 'vanity' in Latin), including flowers, riches and art. The artist included herself among the symbolic paraphernalia: her face appears several times as a fleeting reflection of reality in the shiny gold surface of the goblet on the right. The hidden self-portraits also function as a kind of artistic self-advertisement. No other painter employed this virtuoso device as frequently as Peeters; indeed, it was through her that it became a widespread feature of still-life painting.

Such self-portraits constitute the only record of Peeters, a painter whose personal circumstances remain a mystery. It is known for certain neither where she lived nor when she died. Her training and her circle of patrons are the subject of speculation. Her name appears in no list of members of a painters' guild in the Netherlands – although the lists in Antwerp, where she probably worked, have not survived in their entirety for the period concerned. Not even her date of birth can be established beyond doubt. If she is identical with the Clara Peeters who was baptized on 15 May 1594 in the Antwerp church of St Walburga, then she was barely fourteen years old when she created her first, masterly still lifes. Judging by the signed and dated pictures by her that have survived, her career as a successful painter lasted at least twenty years. One thing is clear: she must have been a very strong artistic personality to have exerted such a decisive influence on still-life painting, a genre then in its infancy. Peeters's early fish and hunting pieces, for instance, belong among the first pictures of this kind. In the eighteenth and nineteenth centuries still life was to become a speciality of women artists, both professional and amateur, but in the early days of the genre in the Netherlands Peeters was its only female practitioner of note.

Clara Peeters
b. no later than *c.* 1594
d. after 1630 in the Netherlands

- *probably a pupil of the still-life painter Osias Beert in Antwerp*
- *executed still lifes of fish, game, and flowers as well as 'vanitas' paintings*
- *more than 30 surviving signed works, another 70 are attributed to the artist*
- *influential Dutch still-life painter*

Clara Peeters
Still Life with Flowers and Golbets, 1612
Oil on panel, 61 x 49 cm
Staatliche Kunsthalle, Karlsruhe

above
Judith Leyster, *Self-portrait,* c. 1630
Oil on canvas, 75 x 66 cm. National Gallery of Art, Washington, DC

opposite
Judith Leyster, *Joyful Company,* 1630
Oil on canvas, 68 x 57 cm. Musée du Louvre, Paris

Judith Leyster

Perhaps it was fortunate for Judith Leyster that her father went bankrupt in 1625. The once wealthy Haarlem brewer was now forced to find other ways of providing for his nine children, and it may well have made better economic sense for him to have his artistically gifted daughter trained as a painter than to pay a dowry for her. Hitherto, no woman had been a member of the painters' guild in Haarlem, but the respected portrait painter Frans Pieter de Grebber employed his daughter Maria in his work-shop, and it was probably there that the young Judith Leyster, who must have been roughly the same age as Maria, received her first training. More important to her in artistic terms was the influence of Frans Hals, whose virtuoso brushwork and bold compositions created a sensation in the northern Netherlands.

At the age of twenty-four Leyster is docu-mented as a fully fledged painter in the list of members of the Haarlem guild. Like her male counterparts, she trained apprentices in her workshop. A few years previously the painters of Haarlem had made their guild regulations more rigorous so as to maintain the high quality of local art. Whoever wished to set up a workshop had to have trained for a minimum of three years with a recognized master and, following an additional apprenticeship, was required to submit a test piece. Leyster proba-bly submitted the self-portrait reproduced here.

No previous woman artist had gazed so confidently at the viewer as Leyster does in this painting. Relaxed and self-assured, she leans back from the canvas on the easel, resting her arm casually on the back of the chair in such a way that it invades the space occupied by the spectator. The carefully calculated pose betrays not a trace of feminine modesty, none of the decorous restraint characteristic of self-portraits by her elder female colleagues, who always hold their elbows close to the body as befitted a woman of breeding. Leyster shows here that she had learned her lessons from Hals. Like him, she grants the image dynamism through a seemingly spontaneous turn of the body. The drapery reveals full command of Hals's type of bold, free brushwork, and the facial features are rendered with the delicate precision likewise associ-ated with him. Con-temporaries particularly admired the kind of illu-sionism represented by the artist's right hand, which appears almost tangibly close to the viewer. She grasps her brush with a lightness echoing that with which the young man in the painting on the easel holds the bow of his fiddle. These parallel gestures attest to the artist's skill, and educated viewers of the time may well have recognized in them a reference to the age-old dispute concerning the relative merits of painting and music. Moreover, the artist appears to be speaking, and this suggests a stock feature of writing on the visual arts since Antiquity: a human image was said to be so lifelike that it could almost be heard to speak.

This self-portrait was long thought to be a major painting by Hals. Leyster's pictures were often confused with Hals's in her own lifetime, and only gradually has her work been rescued from false attributions. The name Leyster means 'lodestar', and the artist frequently referred to this by adding a star to the mono-gram 'JL' with which she signed her paintings.

Judith Leyster
b. 1609 Haarlem, Holland
d. 1660 Haarlem, Holland

- *influenced by Frans Hals, she produced powerful genre paintings*
- *only about 20 works survive*
- *first woman admitted to the Haarlem painters' guild, in 1633*
- *had three pupils in 1635*

Elisabetta Sirani

In the eyes of her contemporaries Elisabetta Sirani of Bologna was the ideal woman artist – young, beautiful and unmarried, gifted, pious and, despite her success, modest of manner. She drew and painted with an ease and a speed that drew astonished admirers to her studio. She gave her images the softness, elegance and decorous beauty that, since the Renaissance, had been deemed the natural expression of femininity. Not least, her work accorded with the dominant taste of the time for the style of Guido Reni, a painter all but worshipped in seventeenth-century Italy.

The artist's father, Giovanni Andrea Sirani, had worked as Reni's assistant and inherited some of his teacher's drawings and composition studies. Giovanni recognized Elisabetta's outstanding talent for drawing only after his attention had repeatedly been drawn to it by his friend the art critic Count Carlo Cesare Malvasia. Sirani himself taught his daughter and, when arthritis eventually forced him to give up painting, made her head of his workshop. Although henceforth she provided for the entire family, she was still required to pass on all her earnings to her father. Soon, she was instructing not only her two sisters, Barbara and Anna Maria, but also a number of other young women. More than a dozen women painters are known to have belonged to Sirani's circle.

Sirani was exceptionally prolific, producing almost two hundred works over a period of thirteen years. Only with the help of her assistants was she in a position to carry out all her commissions, so it is scarcely surprising that her pictures vary considerably in quality. The bulk of her work, in addition to portraits and mythological subjects, consists of religious paintings. She herself produced engravings of these. Most frequently represented among them are images of the Virgin and Child and the Holy Family, popular subjects that she invested with the character of intimate family scenes notable for naturalistic depictions of a playful Christ Child. An example is the painting illustrated here, which, with its exquisite colour harmonies and gently flowing brushwork, belongs among Sirani's finest.

The catalogue that Sirani made of her work breaks off after 182 entries, following the celebrated artist's death in August 1665 at the age of twenty-seven. She had suffered for months from stomach pains, and the most extraordinary rumours circulated after her death. Her servant was accused of poisoning her, but the autopsy carried out in connection with the servant's trial revealed a stomach ulcer. Some scholars now believe that Sirani died of overwork. Her fame was not affected by her early death. The artist, who had been a full member of the Accademia di San Luca in Rome, was accorded an official burial by the Bolognese authorities, and just over ten years later the first biography of her was published. In this, her 'discoverer', Count Malvasia, traced a tradition of women artists in the city, from the painter–saint Catherine of Bologna, via the Renaissance sculptor Properzia dei Rossi and the famous painter Lavinia Fontana, to contemporary times. Never before and nowhere else in Europe had there been so many women artists active in a single place as in Bologna in the sixteenth and seventeenth centuries.

Elisabetta Sirani
b. 8 January 1638 Bologna
d. 1665 Bologna

- *trained under her father, Giovanni Andrea Sirani, a pupil of Guido Reni*
- *member of the Accademia di San Luca, Rome*
- *had numerous female pupils*
- *left an extensive body of work of varying quality*
- *maintained ties with musicians and writers of the day*

Elisabetta Sirani
Virgin and Child, 1663
Oil on canvas, 86.4 x 69.9 cm
National Museum of Women in the Arts, Washington, DC

Maria Sibylla Merian

It is early in the year 1702. In the 'Rose Branch', her house in Amsterdam's Kerkstraat, Maria Sibylla Merian is at work on a book about flora and fauna in the Dutch colony Surinam in South America. Carefully mixing the top-quality watercolours she has made herself, she uses the finest of brushes to paint exotic sprays of flowers in yellow and orange on a large sheet of the most expensive parchment. She depicts caterpillars crawling over the leaves and stems with the same exactitude as the firmly spun cocoons from which she shows butterflies and moths emerging with delicately shaded wings.

The previous autumn Merian had returned from a study trip to Surinam – at the time an extremely hazardous undertaking for a woman, especially one over fifty years old. She and her daughter Dorothea had spent two years in the hot and humid climate sketching beetles, flowers, leaves, caterpillars, butterflies and reptiles until they almost dropped dead from exhaustion. These studies from nature now formed the basis of artistic compositions. In these the viewer's attention is always drawn to an exotic plant with colourful flowers, fruit and large leaves, but the artist's own interest was insects, which she depicted lifesize at every stage of their development. Nothing of the kind had been seen before in Europe. Scientists and enthusiasts had already collected specially preserved specimens of exotic insects for their chambers of curiosities, but Merian presented them not as dead objects but as living creatures metamorphosing in their natural environment.

Metamorphosis Insectorum Surinamensium (The Metamorphosis of the Insects of Surinam) was Merian's magnum opus, for which she spared no expense or effort. Sixty printing plates were engraved in the original size after her watercolours, and she herself wrote commentaries and descriptions that included discussion of the indigenous population's way of life. By this time Merian was already well known. In her first publication, *Blumenbuch* (Flower Book) of 1675, she provided naturalistic models for embroidery and painting on cloth, which were popular activities among burghers' wives at the time. Her second book, a volume on caterpillars entitled *Der Raupen wunderbare Verwandlung und sonderbare Blumennahrung* of 1679, attracted the attention of naturalists and scholars.

The metamorphosis of the plain caterpillar into the resplendent butterfly had fascinated Merian ever since her childhood in Frankfurt am Main. Stimulated by a visit to a local silkworm breeder, she began collecting and classifying insects in cardboard boxes. The daughter of a respected publisher and engraver, Matthäus Merian the Elder, she grew up in a cultivated environment. Following the early death of her father, she acquired knowledge of artistic techniques from her stepfather, Jacob Marrel, an experienced still-life painter. Since guild regulations in Frankfurt did not permit women to practise oil painting, she concentrated on watercolour and learned engraving. She married the moderately successful architectural painter Johann Andreas Graff while still young, but continued her scientific and artistic activities unabated. The marriage appears not to have been happy: the couple separated twenty years later, and Merian and her two daughters joined a strict religious community in the Netherlands. All her work had been informed by a profound Christian faith, which led her to recognize the presence of God in even the tiniest insect. To this day, the precision of her images and their artistic quality have lost none of their power to captivate the viewer.

Maria Sibylla Merian
b. 2 April 1647 Frankfurt am Main
d. 13 January 1717 Amsterdam

- *daughter of the engraver Matthäus Merian the Elder, studied under her stepfather, the still-life painter Jacob Marrel*
- *ran a school in Nuremberg for women flower painters*
- *an expert on insects and the only notable German painter of flowers and animals in the 17th century*

Maria Sibylla Merian
Eriythrina glauca et Arsenura armida Cr., 1700–1702
Water- and body colour on parchment, 40.0 x 30.5 cm
St Petersburg Academy of Sciences, St Petersburg

Rachel Ruysch

Rachel Ruysch's career as a successful artist lasted over sixty-five years. She was the last major exponent of Dutch still-life painting, rivalled as a flower painter only by Jan van Huysum. Her pictures were already greatly sought-after and fetched high prices during her lifetime, and their desirability increased by the fact that only a few left her studio every year. Today there are paintings by her in most of the world's major museums. Ruysch remained true to her chosen subject matter throughout her career, creating ever new variations on flower and fruit still lifes of an unparalleled richness and luminosity. Ruysch's patrons valued the decorative character of her still lifes as much as their naturalistic precision.

Ruysch was an exception to the rule that most women who embraced an artistic career were able to do so because their fathers were painters. She grew up in a cosmopolitan Amsterdam household in which science loomed large. Her father, Frederik Ruysch, a respected botanist and professor of anatomy, no doubt awakened his daughter's interest in the world of flora and fauna early in life. He fostered her artistic talent, paying for her to receive instruction from the well-known still-life painter Willem van Aelst at the age of fifteen. No other studio in Amsterdam could have provided better training. Here, Ruysch learned an excellent painting technique and became acquainted with the latest developments in still-life painting. Van Aelst distributed the objects in his flower and hunting pieces asymmetrically on the picture plane, generating a sense of drama that contrasted with the more regular arrangements characteristic of painters of the older generation. Ruysch adopted her teacher's style of composition.

For the flower piece reproduced here Ruysch chose a relatively small number of items: sumptuous white and pink roses, an exquisite pale violet iris, a carnation with flamelike markings, wild flowers such as a red poppy and a blue field bindweed, and an ear of corn. Like all professional still-life painters, she did not paint such a collection of objects from nature but drew on her store of individual studies. At first sight, the arrangement may seem rather haphazard, but still lifes like this were carefully composed down to the last detail. The viewer's eye is drawn to the full, light-coloured roses in the centre; stems spread outwards from here in a series of S-shaped curves, some extending as far as the edge of the picture. The artist makes skilful use of contrast, setting off dense against loose areas, broad leaves against thin stalks, cold colours against warm. The coloured flowers emerge from the dark background like actors making their entrance on a stage, with light used subtly to create a strong three-dimensional quality.

When she painted this picture, in 1698, the artist was thirty-four years old and had been married to the painter Juriaen Pool for five years. She had given birth to her first child three years previously; nine further children followed, but she did not reduce her artistic activity as a result. Ruysch's career reached its climax in 1708, when she was made court painter in Düsseldorf by Johann Wilhelm, the Elector Palatine. She painted her last picture, a flower piece now in the Musée des Beaux-Arts, Lille, in 1747 at the age of eighty-three.

Rachel Ruysch
b. 1663/64 The Hague or Amsterdam
d. 12 October 1750 Amsterdam

- *trained under the still-life painter Willem van Aelst*
- *in 1701 member of the painters' guild in The Hague*
- *from 1708 to 1716 court painter to Johann Wilhelm, the Elector Palatine, in Düsseldorf*
- *probably corresponded with Maria S. Merian and the leading still life painter Maria Oosterwijk*

Rachel Ruysch
Flowers in a Bulbous Vase, 1698
Oil on canvas, 58 x 44 cm
Städelsches Kunstinstitut, Frankfurt am Main

The Eighteenth Century

Rosalba Carriera

Giulia Lama

Anna Dorothea Therbusch

Angelica Kauffmann

Anne Vallayer-Coster

Adélaïde Labille-Guiard

Elisabeth Vigée-Lebrun

France set the tone in cultural matters in eighteenth-century Europe. The latest vogues at the royal court of Versailles and in the salons of Paris were soon being imitated everywhere. People spoke, wrote and thought French, and they built and painted in the French style, whether at the princely courts of Germany, in the palaces of Venice or at the court of Catherine the Great in Russia. A more intimate type of art, decorative and light-hearted, replaced the pathos of the Baroque style.

The arts as practised at royal courts during the Rococo period encompassed everything from architecture to fashion. This was a fantastical realm of extravagant luxury and sophisticated elegance. In paintings notable for their free brushwork and light colours artists such as Jean-Honoré Fragonard and François Boucher captured the gallantry of the pastoral games played by the aristocracy – a world in which women were idolized and seduced by male admirers who themselves acted with light-footed elegance. In Italy Giambattista Tiepolo created colourful frescoes that formed a splendid background for glittering festivities, and even his religious paintings resemble lavish stage performances.

Towards the end of the century the courtly world of the Rococo had come to epitomize decadence. A new current of intellectual thought known as the Enlightenment blossomed in England (John Locke) and Scotland (David Hume) that would fundamentally change European culture and society. Voltaire, Diderot, Rousseau, Kant and other scholars emphasized reason and individualism, and in so doing questioned the long-established authority of the church, the monarchy and the state. The American Declaration of Independence of 1776 made Enlightenment ideas the basis of a new political order, while in France the thirst for liberty, equality and fraternity led in 1789 to revolution. The French people drove the royal family from their palaces, proclaimed the rights of man and established a republic, which lasted until a military leader – Napoleon – set himself up as head of state and called himself emperor. The French Revolution did not automatically bring improvements in the status of women. They continued to be denied political rights under the republican constitution, and things stayed that way under Napoleon: 'Men are the protectors of their wives; women owe obedience to their husbands.'

above left
Jean-Antoine Watteau
Embarkation for Cythera,
c. 1718
Oil on canvas, 44.3 x 54.4 cm
Städelsches Kunstinstitut,
Frankfurt am Main

above centre
Giambattista Tiepolo
The Education of the Virgin,
1732
Oil on canvas, 362 x 200 cm
Santa Maria della Consolazione (Fava), Venice

above right
François Boucher
Nude Girl (Louison O'Murphy), 1752
Oil on canvas, 59 x 73 cm
Alte Pinakothek, Munich

The neoclassical painter Jacques-Louis David became the leading artist of the French Revolution. His *Oath of the Horatii* of 1784-85 epitomizes civic courage and republican thinking. The painting embodies the artistic ideals of neoclassicism in its clear forms, its Antique subject and its high moral tone. Neoclassicism had appeared around mid-century in opposition to the prevailing Rococo style. In their writings the painter Anton Raphael Mengs and the scholar Johann Joachim Winckelmann invoked Classical Antiquity as a cultural model. Sensational discoveries at Pompeii, Rome and Herculaneum fed a reawakened interest in archaeology. In Germany, the great poet Johann

Jacques-Louis David
The Oath of the Horatii,
1784-85
Oil on canvas, 330 x 425 cm
Musée du Louvre, Paris

Wolfgang von Goethe was infected by this enthusiasm for the Ancient world and, like countless artists, scholars and noblemen, undertook the 'Grand Tour' to Italy. In the German artists' colony in Rome he met Angelica Kauffmann, whose paintings on Classical subjects are notable for elegance of form and emotional sensitivity. Kauffmann's work was enthusiastically received throughout Europe.

Opportunities for women continued to be restricted by law and convention in the eighteenth century, but the cultural climate during both the Rococo period and the subsequent middle-class age of 'sensibility' at least favoured any artistic ambitions they may have entertained. The mainspring of all artistic pleasure and creation was thought to lie in human feeling – an area in which women were generally held to be especially at home. There were many amateur women artists, active in the fields of miniatures, portraits, still lifes and pastel. Some women, such as Kauffmann, Rosalba Carriera and Elisabeth Vigée-Lebrun, achieved a degree of artistic fame and influence unknown to any of their predecessors, and their reputation lived on after their death. The vast majority, however, could not become official practitioners, because women were excluded from art academies.

Academies played a decisive role in eighteenth-century art. Gradually, they supplanted the old painters' guilds in all the large cities of Europe. Not only did the academies provide sound training; they were also centres of debate on theoretical matters and arbiters of taste. Furthermore, as royal institutions under the patronage of heads of state, they served to increase the status of the arts and of their members. In Paris, only members of the Academy were permitted to contribute work to an exhibition shown every two years in the Salon Carrée at the Louvre. This exhibition – known as the Salon – was the major artistic event in eighteenth-century Paris. Everyone who was anybody flocked to the Salon to admire and discuss the paintings, which were hung very close together. The highest-ranking genre was history painting – images that depicted exemplary figures and stories from Christian iconography and Classical literature and mythology. History painting demanded of the artist skill in invention, which was valued far more highly than the ability 'merely' to reproduce the visible world. After history painting came portraiture, genre painting (scenes from everyday life), landscape and still life in the official academic hierarchy of subjects, which remained valid until well into the nineteenth century.

Women Artists and the Academies

Art academies were a male preserve. Only in exceptional cases – as a result of royal intervention, for example – did a successful woman artist become an honorary member of an Academy. The Academy in Paris, for instance, numbered some 450 men among its members between its foundation in the seventeenth century and the French Revolution, but only fifteen women – and most of those were wives or daughters of members. In 1783 the number of women members was officially restricted to four. At a sitting of Academy members held after the Revolution the portraitist Adélaïde Labille-Guiard put forward a motion calling for the abolition of membership restrictions for women. Although the motion was passed, a short time later the Academy resolved not to admit any women at all.

Women were largely excluded not only from academic honours, but also from academic training. This meant that they lacked the knowledge and technique necessary to practise the highest-ranking pictorial genre, history painting, which was grounded in skills taught at the Academies: drawing from Antique sculptures, copying Old Masters and studying the naked human body. It is thus no accident that the eighteenth century brought forth a number of fine women portrait painters but scarcely a single woman history painter.

Marguerite Gérard
Bad News, 1789
Oil on canvas, 63 x 50 cm
Musée du Louvre, Paris

This state of affairs did not prevent the ambitious portraitist Elisabeth Vigée-Lebrun from submitting a history painting (an allegory entitled *Peace Bringing Back Plenty*) as her test piece on the occasion of her admission to the Academy in 1783. Other women likewise responded resourcefully to the challenge of adverse conditions. Angelica Kauffmann, for instance, used subtle painterly means to compensate for her lack of anatomical knowledge and also concentrated on female figures, which were easier for her to study. As a founding member of the Royal Academy of Arts in London, she supported the English artist Maria Cosway, who achieved considerable success with strongly emotional subjects drawn from Classical mythology and literature. Even an acknowledged portrait painter such as Marie-Geneviève Bouliar once ventured to tackle a subject from antiquity in the form of an imaginary portrait of Aspasia of Miletus, the lover of the Athenian statesman Pericles. By contrast, her French contemporary Marguerite Gérard, sister-in-law of the Rococo painter Jean-Honoré Fragonard, specialized in elegant images of everyday life among the upper classes. One of France's most successful women painters, Gérard never belonged to the Academy.

From 1791 the Salon exhibitions in Paris were open to painters who were not members of the Academy. This represented an important step forward for women artists because it meant that they could now show work at the Salon. The numbers who did so increased from year to year. The fact that respected or famous artists such as Jacques-Louis David und Jean-Baptiste Greuze now accepted female students also contributed towards the acceptance of women artists in society.

Events in History: The Eighteenth Century

1723
Johann Sebastian Bach becomes cathedral choirmaster in Leipzig.

1735
Swedish naturalist Carolus Linnaeus (Carl von Linné) develops a new system of classification for plants.

1738
John and Charles Wesley and George Whitefield start the Methodist movement in the Church of England.

1751-72
Denis Diderot and Jean-Baptiste d'Alembert publish the *Encyclopédie ou dictionnaire raisonné des sciences*.

1773
With the 'Boston Tea Party', the sinking of several shiploads of tea in Boston Harbor, North American settlers revolt against England's colonial policy.

1776
The thirteen American colonies declare their independence from England.

1781
Immanuel Kant publishes his philosophical treatise *The Critique of Pure Reason*.

1789
Outbreak of the French Revolution. George Washington becomes first President of the United States.

1804
Napoleon Bonaparte crowns himself Emperor of France. The *Code Napléon, or Civil Code*, is issued.

Rosalba Carriera

Rosalba Carriera was fifty-five years old when she portrayed herself as Winter, wearing a fur hat and a white fur collar that provide a soft frame for rather severe features. The disguise has not been adopted playfully: the artist gazes at the viewer soberly, seriously. The cool grey-blue colours recall those of the time of year she is personifying. In the course of her career Carriera often painted the four seasons in the shape of beautiful young girls – the kind of light-hearted symbolism popular during the Rococo. This is the only occasion on which she lent an allegorical figure her own features. In choosing winter, she was not only referring to her advancing years but also revealing a melancholy side to her character. Later, when Carriera's sister died and she herself became blind she succumbed to depression.

This Venetian was among the most successful women artists of her day. Her portraits and allegories were admired throughout Europe. Royalty and members of the aristocracy, including the King of Denmark, the Elector Palatine Johann Wilhelm and Maximilian II of Bavaria, all but queued up outside her studio to have their portraits painted. August II of Saxony acquired more than 150 works by Carriera, which are now in the Gemäldegalerie in Dresden. To enter the gallery there that contains her pastel portraits is to be confronted by the image of an entire epoch: whether coquettish, reserved, vain, friendly, charming or dignified, these ladies and gentlemen of court society always exude an air

above
Rosalba Carriera
The Dancer Barbarina, c. 1739
Pastel on paper, 56.5 x 46.5 cm
Staatliche Kunstsammlung Dresden,
Gemäldegalerie Alte Meister, Dresden

Rosalba Carriera
Self-portrait as Winter, 1731
Pastel on paper, 46.5 x 34 cm
Staatliche Kunstsammlung Dresden,
Gemäldegalerie Alte Meister, Dresden

of sophistication and elegance. Carriera portrayed her contemporaries as they wanted to appear. Though she catered to their taste for modish elegance, she did not idealize them indiscriminately, for she possessed a remarkable ability to capture the individuality of her sitters.

The dancer Barbarina, whom Carriera painted around 1740, was an international celebrity. Born in Parma, she was acclaimed as a dancer in Paris and London. Frederick the Great engaged her to appear at his opera house in Berlin, where the Grand Chancellor Samuel von Cocceji once proposed to her on stage. The artist indicates Barbarina's profession by depicting her in the animated pose of a dancer. The porcelain-like fineness of her skin, the precious jewellery, the delicate silk bows, the flowers and the lace of the Rococo dress are rendered with consummate skill.

Both these portraits are rendered not in oils, but in pastel on paper. Two hundred years earlier Leonardo da Vinci had already experimented with this medium, which consists of dry pigments mixed with gum binder and made into sticks for drawing. Carriera, who was introduced to pastel by an English art lover after she had made a name for herself as a painter of miniatures, brought the medium to new heights of technical virtuosity and was responsible for its popularity spreading throughout Europe. After she visited Paris, for example, the French painters Maurice-Quentin de La Tour and Jean-Etienne Liotard adopted pastel, as did many amateur women artists, with whom it remained a favoured medium until well into the nineteenth century.

Rosalba Carriera
b. 7 October 1675 Venice
d. 1757 Venice

- *maintained ties with artists such as Antonio Balestra and Federico Bencovich*
- *honorary member of the Academies of Rome, Bologna and Paris*
- *Paris sojourn from 1720 to 1721; one of her subjects was Jean-Antoine Watteau*
- *outstanding pastelist, who influenced painters such as Maurice-Quentin de La Tour, Jean-Etienne Liotard, Anton Raffael Mengs*

Giulia Lama

I've just discovered a woman here who paints better than Rosalba [Carriera] when it comes to large-scale compositions… In her youth she studied mathematics with the famous Pater Maffei. The painters give the poor woman a rough time, but her talent triumphs over her foes. True, she is as ugly as she is intelligent, but she talks in a charming and polished manner, so it is easy to forgive her face. (She also makes embroideries and has devoted much thought to a machine … that could make lace mechanically.) But she lives a very secluded life.' This description of the Venetian painter Giulia Lama was penned by Abbot Luigi Conti in a letter of 1 March 1728. She was thirty-seven years old at the time and must already have enjoyed a reputation as an artist in her home town.

Lama was completely forgotten after her death. Paintings by her were attributed to Jan Lyss, Giambattista Piazzetta, Francisco de Zurbarán and other contemporaries, until scholars in recent years rehabilitated her as one of the leading women artists of the eighteenth century. Most of her work has disappeared, but the few surviving paintings bear witness to a bold, individual artistic personality. To become acquainted with her art it is necessary to travel to Venice. Her 1722 painting of the Virgin and Child accompanied by saints has graced the high altar of the Renaissance church of Sta Maria Formosa for almost three hundred years. The parish registers record that she was born here in 1681 to the painter Agostino Lama and died here on 7 October 1747. That is the sum total of documentary evidence relating to Giulia Lama. A major work by her, a Crucifixion of Christ, hangs in S. Vidal, a small church not far from the Canal Grande that is no longer used as a place of worship. The side altars still bear six large-format paintings created around 1730 by some of the finest artists in Venice. In this company, which includes the greatly esteemed Sebastiano Ricci

and other painters of the older generation, Lama and Giambattista Piazzetta represent the Venetian avant-garde of the day, their images notable for a dramatic use of light and shade. Lama used to be thought of as Piazzetta's pupil, but both were roughly the same age and, as the children of artists, may have known each other from an early age. Certainly, they were later in close contact and influenced each other artistically. Their relationship became the subject of gossip, but all we now have to go on is the striking portrait that Piazzetta painted of Lama in 1728.

Works by Lama and Piazzetta can again be compared not far from S. Vidal, in the Accademia, which contains what is probably Lama's best-known painting, *Judith and Holofernes*. A century earlier, the Baroque painter Artemisia Gentileschi had depicted the killing that lies at the centre of this biblical tale, and in the most drastic manner. By contrast, Lama chose to represent a moment before the deed is done. The powerful body of the naked Assyrian general lies in the foreground. Its unnatural twist, the suggestion of flickering light and the dramatic juxtapositions of light and shade generate a mood of foreboding. For a last time, Judith turns in prayer to God – a moment later she will grab the sword hanging in the half-light at the back and behead the enemy commander. Holofernes's body is exposed, defenceless, to the gaze of the viewer.

Giulia Lama
b. 1 October 1681 Venice
d. 7 October 1747 Venice

- *possibly trained under the Venetian artist Antonio Molinari*
- *around 200 surviving charcoal drawings, including male nudes*
- *like her contemporary Giambattista Piazzetta, she executed large and dramatic altarpieces and biblical scenes*
- *her self-portrait is on display in the Uffizi portrait gallery*

Giulia Lama
Judith and Holofernes, c. 1730
Oil on canvas, 107 x 155 cm
Galleria dell'Accademia, Venice

Anna Dorothea Therbusch

Berlin was far from being an artistic centre of international standing in the first half of the eighteenth century. The names of most painters then active in the Prussian capital are now familiar only to specialists. One of them was the Polish émigré Georg Lisiewski, who painted military portraits during the reign of the 'soldier king' Frederick William I. Lisiewski had three children whose reputations as artists exceeded his own: Christian Friedrich Reinhold, Anna Rosina and Anna Dorothea, the youngest daughter and the best known of the three.

Anna Dorothea Lisiewski's hopes of becoming an artist suffered a setback when she married a Berlin innkeeper by the name of Therbusch at the age of twenty-one. Childbirth followed, and a life led under the strict surveillance of her mother-in-law offered no opportunities to study painting. She never lost sight of her goal, however, and proceeded to teach herself, re-entering the public arena as a portrait painter when she was over forty. In 1761 she is documented at the court in Stuttgart as a painter of decorative mythological scenes and was subsequently appointed court painter in Mannheim.

Encouraged by her success, Therbusch set off for Paris, the leading centre of the visual arts in Europe. She did so without patronage and without the benefit of connections among influential people – an extremely bold undertaking for a woman whose husband in Berlin was a low-ranking innkeeper and had correspondingly modest means at his disposal. She experienced difficulties establishing herself in Paris, but by 1767 had become successful enough to be made a member of the Academy. One contemporary commentator remarked sarcastically that in accepting Madame Therbusch the Academy certainly could not be accused of being over-susceptible to female charms, for the new member was neither young nor beautiful. She showed work at the Salon and found a supporter in the famous philosopher and writer on art Denis Diderot. Paris was expensive, however, and lucrative commissions were in short supply. Debt eventually forced her to leave the city. 'She did not lack the talent necessary to create a sensation in this country', wrote Diderot. 'She lacked youth, beauty, modesty and coquetry.'

Back in Berlin, the widely travelled artist could be sure of public attention (and nobody could tell whether she was really entitled to append 'Peintre du Roy de France' [painter to the King of France] to her signature). She did work for Frederick the Great and produced portraits of high-ranking members of society, both aristocratic and non-aristocratic.

Among her finest paintings is the self-portrait reproduced here, which she created a few years before her death. Although it is not uniformly detailed in execution, it in no way appears unfinished. Therbusch depicts herself as an educated woman, holding an open book. She calmly scrutinizes us through an eyeglass hanging down over her forehead. Her contemporary Jean-Baptiste-Siméon Chardin painted himself wearing spectacles and an eye-shade, but for a woman who lived in an age that made a fetish of female beauty to produce such a portrait was remarkable indeed. She could easily have left out the eyeglass, but instead she takes advantage of this 'ugly' appurtenance to focus the viewer's attention on her eye as the vehicle of her art. For all its apparent modesty, the portrait reflects the confidence and self-awareness of a woman who had had to overcome many obstacles.

Anna Dorothea Therbusch
b. 23 July 1721 Berlin
d. 9 November 1782 Berlin

- *trained under her father, Georg Lisiewski*
- *influenced by Antoine Pesne and Jean-Antoine Watteau*
- *her surviving oeuvre comprises more than 200 oils, pastels and drawings*
- *she had a studio in Berlin from 1773*
- *executed paintings on mythological subjects for Frederick the Great and the court of the tsars*

Anna Dorothea Therbusch
Self-portrait, 1776-77
Oil on canvas, 151 x 115 cm
Gemäldegalerie, Berlin

Angelica Kauffmann

Angelica Kauffmann was immensely gifted and was encouraged at an early age to develop her artistic talent. She executed a self-portrait in oils when she was twelve and, at the age of sixteen, used engravings as a basis for large-format paintings of the Apostles that she created for a church in her native Switzerland. Her father, a minor painter, soon realized that he had nothing more to teach his daughter. He travelled with her to Italy in order to acquaint her with the best models and foster her career. There, she copied paintings in the great collections and made contact with patrons of the arts and fellow painters from around Europe.

Kauffmann painted this portrait of the schoolar Johann Joachim Winckelmann in 1764 in Rome. Winckelmann, who administered the Vatican collection of antiquities, had acquired a reputation far beyond the boundaries of Italy for his writings on the art of Classical Antiquity. The commission to paint his portrait was a godsend for the twenty-two-year-old artist, who benefited from the fame of her sitter and his widespread connections. A contemporary wrote of the portrait: 'Angelica's Winckelmann is a masterpiece in its colour, pose, harmony, drawing and power.' The subtle colour composition and the gentle features are typical of Kauffmann's work, and she was later to be severely criticized for making the great German poet Johann Wolfgang von Goethe look 'effeminate' in her portrait of him. This in no way harmed her friendship with the slightly younger Goethe.

Generally, it was the very softness, gracefulness and gently elegiac mood of Kauffmann's paintings that drew the approval of her contemporaries, for whom they embodied the artistic ideal of 'sensibility'. In creating her history paintings, in which women frequently play a major role, she succeeded in entering an almost exclusively male domain. It was a precondition of her outstanding success as an artist that her works and her personality accorded perfectly with contemporary notions of femininity.

In *Self-portrait Hesitating between the Arts of Music and Painting* she shows herself reluctantly bidding farewell to Music, personified by a female figure crowned with a wreath of flowers, and turning to Painting, who points energetically to a temple of fame in the distance. In her youth Kauffmann had toyed with the idea of pursuing a career as a singer, and in this painting she transforms this episode in her life into an ambitious, complex history painting that contains references to two Classical subjects: Hercules at the Crossroads and the Three Graces.

Kauffmann spent a large part of her life in Rome and in London, where her house became a centre of social activity. Among the few women of her time to acquire considerable wealth from the pursuit of an artistic career, she was extremely prolific until shortly before her death. She produced approximately five hundred portraits and countless history paintings. Elected to the Academies in Bologna, Florence and Rome, she was founding member of the Royal Academy of Arts in London, which thereafter did not accept another woman as member until 1923.

Angelica Kauffmann
b. 30 October 1741 Chur Switzerland
d. 5 November 1807 Rome

- *moved to London in 1766, where she became a founding member of the Royal Academy of Arts*
- *after 1781, lived in Italy with her second husband, the painter Antonio Zucchi*
- *first biography of her, published in 1810, shortly after her death*
- *a celebrated and highly paid artist who was not forgotten after her death*

Angelica Kauffmann
Self-portrait Hesitating between the Arts of Music and Painting, c. 1794
Oil on canvas, 147 x 216 cm
Nostell Priory, Wakefield, Yorkshire

opposite
Angelica Kauffmann
Portrait of Johann Joachim Winckelmann, 1764
Oil on canvas, 97.2 x 71.0 cm
Kunsthaus Zurich, Zurich

Anne Vallayer-Coster

Here is a ham to whet the appetite! A knife has already been used to start cutting a slice of the juicy meat with its generous layer of fat and brown crust. A sprig of laurel, a bunch of fresh radishes, a full-bellied bottle of wine and a carafe of water complete the simple arrangement of objects on a stone surface covered with a white cloth. The eye takes in the contents of this still life at a glance, but the material qualities of the individual items are depicted so exactly and reproduced so fascinatingly in terms of paint that the viewer is continually discovering things to feast his gaze on. The smooth, reflecting glass of the carafe, the leathery appearance of the laurel leaves, the fineness of the radish roots, the matt surface of the stone and the irregular texture of the ham – all this has been keenly observed and rendered with considerable variety in oil colours, sometimes with a fine brush, sometimes with a broad one, sometimes in thick areas, sometimes in thin layers.

This is one of the earliest surviving still lifes by Anne Vallayer-Coster. It clearly reveals the twenty-three-year-old artist's familiarity with the simple still-life arrangements painted by her elder contemporary Jean-Baptiste-Siméon Chardin. Vallayer-Coster's father worked as a goldsmith at the royal Gobelins tapestry factory before setting up on his own in Paris, equipped with a royal licence for the production of medals and other official decorations. Anne Vallayer-Coster undoubtedly benefited from her father's royal connections and was herself later appointed Painter to the Queen. At first she devoted herself to portraiture, but soon found her true métier in still-life painting. She was accepted into the royal Art Academy at the early age of twenty-six – an extremely rare honour for a woman and a decisive step forward in her career. As an Academy member, she was permitted to show work at the Salons in the Louvre, which she did until her death more than forty years later. The philosopher and writer on art Denis Diderot discussed her work in his Salon reviews, which brought her to the attention of a wider group of patrons, most of whom belonged to the aristocracy or influential circles in Paris. Only her portraits were not well received: in this field she was thought inferior to Elisabeth Vigée-Lebrun and Adélaïde Labille-Guiard. In 1781 she was the recipient of a coveted mark of royal favour: along with her husband, she was permitted to join other celebrated artists in occupying a studio and living quarters in the Louvre.

Vallayer-Coster's still lifes encompass a wide range of motifs. Sumptuous bouquets of roses appear in vases of precious porcelain; Antique statues stand next to exotic shells, musical instruments or the attributes of painting; dead hares are decked out as hunting trophies; peaches rise in pyramids from baskets of fruit; steam wafts up from exquisite teacups. The artist remained true to this subject matter. The Revolution swept aside the *ancien régime* and neoclassicism conquered the Salon, but Vallayer-Coster continued to paint what she had always painted: bewitchingly beautiful images of flowers and other objects that delight the eye. Along with Chardin and Jean-Baptiste Oudry she was the finest still-life painter in eighteenth-century France.

Anne Vallayer-Coster
b. 21 December 1744
Gobelins near Paris
d. 28 February 1818 Paris

- *appointed Painter to the Queen by Marie-Antoinette in 1780*
- *oeuvre comprises more than 120 still lifes*
- *the National Gallery in Washington, DC, honoured her with a retrospective in 2002*

Anne Vallayer-Coster
Still Life with Ham, Bottles and Radishes, 1767
Oil on canvas, 45.1 x 53.3 cm
Gemäldegalerie, Berlin

Adélaïde Labille-Guiard

Adélaïde Labille-Guiard
b. 11 April 1749 Paris
d. 24 April 1803 Paris

- *trained under François-André Vincent and Maurice Quentin de La Tour, among others*
- *after the Revolution, she painted portraits of the leading men in the National Assembly*
- *always overshadowed by the more famous Elisabeth-Louise Vigée-Lebrun*
- *artist to the 'Mesdames de France', the daughters of Louis XV*

In a self-portrait the painter Adélaïde Labille-Guiard depicted herself dressed in strikingly fashionable clothes among her pupils. At the time, an appearance of this kind was a sine qua non of social acceptance. Labille-Guiard, a resourceful woman with a keen sense of reality, fought for the rights of women artists. As a child, she had observed how high-ranking women fitted themselves out with bows, ribbons and other extravagant accoutrements in her father's elegant haberdashery. Later, as a sought-after portraitist, she excelled at rendering the sheen on silk, the fineness of lace and other features of clothing. Her chief interest, however, lay in the character of her sitters.

Labille-Guiard's father doubtless entertained no thoughts of his daughter becoming a successful artist when he arranged for her to receive training from a nearby miniature painter. Why shouldn't she paint a little to pass the time, like other middle-class girls and noblewomen? She might even be able to make some money by decorating tobacco boxes, medallions and so forth. Adélaïde Labille-Guiard had set her sights higher than this. At the age of twenty, shortly after marrying a finance official, she studied pastel with a great exponent of the medium, the elderly Maurice-Quentin de La Tour. When a friend of her youth, François-André Vincent, returned from a study trip to Italy she decided to learn oil painting from him.

The decisive step in the artistic career of this ambitious woman was her election to the Academy in Paris, which then numbered only two female members: Madame Vien and the still-life painter Anne Vallayer-Coster. Labille-Guiard had proceeded cannily. First, she produced pastel portraits of some Academy members as proof of her ability. Then, on 31 May 1783, she submitted two of these portraits as her test pieces and was accepted by a large majority. At the request of the Queen, Labille-Guiard's keenest rival among women artists, Elisabeth-Louise Vigée-Lebrun, was admitted on the same day. The Academy now included four women among its members. That august institution reacted a short time later by restricting female membership to precisely that number.

The French royal family commissioned Labille-Guiard in 1788 to paint this richly coloured life-size portrait of Princess Louise-Elisabeth of France, who had died thirty years previously – a fact hinted at by the striking shadow on the wall at the right and by the sad expression on the face of her young son. As a result of the turmoil caused by the Revolution the fee of 4,000 *livres* for the picture was never paid and it remained in the possession of the artist, who exhibited it as an anonymous portrait at the Salon of 1791. At that Salon she also showed portraits of Robespierre and other revolutionaries as a way of demonstrating her progressive political sympathies.

Labille-Guiard's hopes that the Revolution would bring about improved opportunities for women artists were soon dashed: in 1793 the reorganized Academy resolved not to admit women at all. In 1795 she and her pupils were at least permitted to occupy artists' quarters in the Louvre, after their request for such rooms had been turned down for years on the grounds that the presence of young women would endanger the morals of the male artists living in the same building.

Adélaïde Labille-Guiard
Portrait of Louise-Elisabeth de France, Duchess of Parma, and her son Ferdinand, 1788
Oil on canvas, 113 x 88.5 cm
Musée National du Château et des Trianons, Versailles

The Nineteenth Century

Constance Mayer

Marie Ellenrieder

Rosa Bonheur

Elizabeth Butler

Berthe Morisot

Mary Cassatt

Camille Claudel

Suzanne Valadon

croix   Carl Spitzweg   Jean-François Millet   Adolph von Menzel   Gustave Courbet   Arnold Böcklin   Dante Gabriel Rossetti   Claude Monet   Vincent van Gogh

Two major trends shaped the debate on art in the nineteenth century. On the one hand, there was a return to the great models of the past. Around 1800, it found expression in neoclassicism and, during the latter half of the century, in variants of historicism. On the other hand, realism and Impressionism looked to the present in search of a new visual language that would express the reality of modern life.

Over the course of the century, the Academies became strongholds of conservative traditions of art, where the careful study of the art of Classical Antiquity, classical rules of composition, a refined painting technique and knowledge of traditional motifs from mythology, literature and history were taught. Academic painters regarded these as the foundations of their art, which turned increasingly rigid with convention, however.

New currents and movements that finally gave rise to modernism were developing on all sides. Essentially, the roots of modern art can be traced back to the time around 1800. While the elegant neoclassicism of Jacques-Louis David and Jean-Auguste-Dominique Ingres still determined the character of official art in France,

Romanticism developed in England and Germany. This was a movement that expressed emotions and irrational tendencies in literature and art. Among its many and diverse manifestations are the fantastic visions of Englishman William Blake and the contemplative landscapes of the German painter Caspar David Friedrich. His landscapes lead the viewer's gaze into a vast, mist-shrouded expanse and allow the spectator room to experience his feelings. Friedrich was not concerned with the reproduction of external reality, but of moods.

French Romanticism took on other characteristics. Eugène Delacroix and Théodore Géricault embraced Baroque use of forms, creating dynamic and passionate monumental paintings that were intended to move and unsettle the viewer. A painting such as Géricault's *The Raft of the Medusa*, which was acclaimed at the 1819 Salon, was based on thorough anatomical studies, detailed drawings and a minutely conceived composition – and thus belonged to a tradition of art that stretched back to the Renaissance.

A quite different approach was taken by a number of landscape painters in the early nineteenth century. They were concerned with capturing their immediate impressions of atmo-

above left
Théodore Géricault
The Raft of the Medusa, 1819
Oil on canvas, 491 x 716 cm
Musée du Louvre, Paris

above centre
Caspar David Friedrich
Chalk Cliffs of Rügen, c. 1818
Oil on canvas, 90.5 x 71 cm
Oskar Reinhart Collection,
Winterthur

above right
Claude Monet
*Wild Poppies near
Argenteuil*, 1873
Oil on canvas, 50 x 65 cm
Musée d'Orsay, Paris

Pierre-Auguste Renoir
Moulin de la Galette, 1876
Oil on canvas, 131 x 175 cm
Musée d'Orsay, Paris

spheric effects and nature in rapidly executed oil studies. In France, the artists of the Barbizon School spent time in the Forest of Fontainebleau and made open-air painting the basis of their art. In England, the landscape painter John Constable employed freer brushstrokes and made use of unconnected blobs of pure colour to render the effect of changing light. The Impressionists followed his approach in the second half of the century. In the shimmering paintings of Claude Monet and Pierre-Auguste Renoir, visible reality is dissolved into individual colour particles that the viewer's eye fuses into an overall impression. These painters no longer looked to literature and history for their subject matter, but to everyday life, be it a summer meadow in the Paris suburbs, the bustle of a street café or railway station, theatregoers or an unknown woman serving behind a bar – these were the aspects of modern life that the painter Edouard Manet and his friend, the novelist Emile Zola, promoted as suitable contemporary motifs.

For the realist Gustave Courbet, even the ugly and the ordinary were worthy subjects. Honoré Daumier drew the poor and the despised, Adolf Menzel factory workers. Nonetheless, images of the reality of the industrial era remained a minor interest. Towards the end of the century, the avant-garde revolution-

ized art with its search for new expressive means. In his passionate landscapes, Vincent van Gogh took the effect of colour to new heights, while Paul Cézanne pioneered a clear and simplified use of forms and painted innumerable variations of the same subject – either a still life of apples or the Mont Saint Victoire.

In the nineteenth century, Paris remained the centre of the art world. Anyone who wanted to get on as an artist went to Paris, the capital of fine art. Railways made it easier and cheaper to get there and exchanges between artists increased. A famous artists' colony evolved in Montmartre, although there were artists living in Paris at the time who never had any contact with its members. Many of today's well-known names, such as Claude Monet, remained outsiders in the art world for quite some time. At the Paris Salon, a massive event with hundreds of paintings on show in dozens of rooms, heart-rending history paintings, sentimental genre scenes and conventional academic allegories were successful year after year. Around mid-century, artists whose work had been refused by the Salon's conservative jury took matters into their own hands: in 1855 Gustave Courbet organized his own exhibition, calling it 'Le Réalisme'. The Impressionists followed his lead two decades later.

Rather than for aristocratic patrons, artists in the nineteenth century worked mainly for the free market, in other words for anonymous buyers. More and more, galleries took the place of direct contact between artist and client. Even during the first half of the century, for instance during the Biedermeier period in Germany (c. 1815–48), bourgeois themes and handy formats determined the character of the art that was being produced. Come the end of the century, too, it was art collectors from the metropolitan bourgeoisie whose purchases supported the avant-garde. Yet the market did not always recognize the significance of some artists, Vincent van Gogh being a prime example of a genius who went unrecognized during his lifetime.

A Turning Point in the History of Women Artists

The nineteenth century saw a sharp increase in the number of women working as artists. While it was still not an everyday occurrence to see a woman painting, it was no longer the rarity it once had been. Even if she had no artistic connections, it was now possible for a woman to find her way into the profession, assuming she could assert herself and had talent, money and a supportive family behind her. For many women, creative ambition came to an end when they married or it did not progress beyond amateur level. It was still the case that a woman who was serious about being a professional artist faced stiff opposition. In the first half of the century, only in a few rare cases did women succeed in gaining admission to public art academies for professional training. Renowned institutions, such as the Ecole des Beaux-Arts in Paris or London's Royal Academy of Arts, generally admitted men only. Nonetheless, towards the end of the eighteenth century, well-known artists started giving private lessons to women, and the first art schools for women soon opened. Other institutions organized separate women's classes. Life drawing for women remained controversial into the second half of the twenti-

Marie Bashkirtseff
In the Studio, 1880-81
Oil on canvas, 185 x 145 cm
Dnipropetrovsk State Art Museum, Dnipropetrovsk

eth century, however. When, in 1897, the Ecole des Beaux-Arts in Paris finally opened its doors to women students, too, the august Academies had long lost their leading position and had become the guardians of conservative tradition.

In the nineteenth century, Rome still attracted large numbers of artists, including the circle of American women sculptors around Harriet Hosmer, who became famous for her monumental neoclassical sculptures. Paris later replaced the Eternal City as the preferred destination of artists,

especially since there were renowned private art schools there, such as the Académies Julian and Colarossi, which also offered classes for women. The Pole Anna Bilinska, the Swiss Louise Breslau, the Swede Hanna Hirsch Pauli and the Dutchwoman Thérèse Schwartze all spent months or years in Paris to continue their training as artists, mostly after having learned the basics in their own country.

The diary of the young Russian Marie Bashkirtseff paints a lively picture of the artistic scene around this time. Many women in Paris experienced a degree of independence they had not previously known, even if they were still unable to move about in public without a chaperone. The opportunities that were open to women to travel and to undergo training had now improved considerably, but that far from guaranteed them a place in the history of art. After their death, most nineteenth-century women artists were quickly forgotten, even if during their lifetime some of them – such as the Dane Anna Ancher or the Norwegian Harriet Backer – were counted among the most important artists of their generation.

Events in History: The Nineteenth Century

1815
Napoleon is defeated and banished to the island of St Helena. The Congress of Vienna introduces the political restoration of Europe.

1824
Ludwig van Beethoven completes his *Ninth Symphony*.

1830
The July Revolution in France leads to the definitive fall of the Bourbons. Opening of the Liverpool-Manchester railway line.

1848
Revolutions in Germany, Austria and France. Karl Marx publishes his *Communist Manifesto*.

1861-65
Slavery is abolished in the United States under President Abraham Lincoln and the secession of the Southern States is prevented by the American Civil War.

1869
Opening of the Suez Canal, for which Giuseppe Verdi composes *Aida* (1870).

1871
After the defeat of France in the Franco-Prussian War, the German Empire is proclaimed in Versailles.

1885
Carl Benz builds the first automobile.

1900
Peak of imperialism. Boxer rebellion in China. Foundation of the Labour Party in England. Civil Code introduced in Germany. Sigmund Freud publishes *Die Traumdeutung* (Interpretation of Dreams).

Constance Mayer

A boat glides soundlessly across pitch-black water. In it, a young woman lies draped in her husband's arms, a sleeping child at her breast. Aided by a small, winged Cupid, a silent female figure vigorously propels the boat through the darkness. In the moonlight, the figures glint as if made of ivory. The sleeping woman is as exquisite as a Venus from Antiquity – and is as motionless as death. One immediately thinks of Charon ferrying the souls of the dead across the rivers Styx and Acheron to Hades. This painting is like a sentimental poem, full of yearning and sadness. When the artist exhibited it at the Paris Salon in 1819, a wordy title provided an explanation of its subject: 'Love and Happiness steer a boat across the river of life. A young man sits in the stern and is shown protecting his wife and sleeping child in his arms.' During the age of neoclassicism, allegorical themes and allusions to Antiquity were held in high regard by art lovers, for whom beautiful, scantily clad female figures could be associated either with love, truth, chastity, decadence or corrupted innocence.

Constance Mayer's own situation was somewhat different from the family idyll shown in her painting. In common with many women of her day, she dreamt of finding happiness in complete devotion to one man. The daughter of a Parisian customs officer, she had studied under the major genre painter Jean-Baptiste Greuze and then worked for a short time in the studio of the celebrated painter Jacques-Louis David, whose heroic style, however, was less suited to her temperament than the elegant and delightful neoclassicism of artist Pierre-Paul Prud'hon, whom she met in 1802. Aged twenty-eight at the time, Mayer had in fact finished training as an artist and had already exhibited her work at the Salon on several occasions. Nonetheless, she wanted to resume studies under Prud'hon, a man seventeen years her senior, and she became his close collaborator, companion and lover. When Prud'hon's

wife was admitted to an institution following a nervous breakdown in 1803, Mayer looked after Prud'hon's children and home. In their work as artists, she was so absorbed in the collaborator she admired and loved that her personality was almost erased from the results of their shared creativity. Her work would even occasionally reach the market under his name. Then again, Prud'hon would draw detailed colour sketches and studies before Mayer executed the painting herself, as in A Dream of Happiness. The idea for it was probably based on a drawing by Mayer's first teacher, Greuze. It was not unusual to borrow other artists' ideas at a time when copying the work of a master formed a large part of an artist's training.

In the end such devoted self-sacrifice brought Mayer neither happiness nor fulfilment. She was overcome by depression and fears for her livelihood, especially when it became clear that Prud'hon was unwilling to marry her after his wife's death. On 27 May 1821 Mayer used a razor to take her own life. Badly shaken, Prud'hon completed her last paintings and mounted a retrospective of her work at the Salon the following year. He himself died in 1823.

Constance Mayer
b. 1775 Paris
d. 26 May 1821 Paris

- *trained under Jean-Baptiste Greuze, Joseph-Benoît Suvée and Jacques-Louis David*
- *executed expressive genre scenes, portraits and allegories*
- *exhibited her work regularly at the Paris Salon after 1796*
- *a representative of classically inspired early 19th century Romanticism*

Constance Mayer
A Dream of Happiness, 1819
Oil on canvas, 97 x 146 cm
Musée du Louvre, Paris

Marie Ellenrieder

Marie Ellenrieder
b. 20 March 1791
Constance
d. 5 June 1863 Constance

- *trained as a miniaturist*
- *first woman to train at the Munich Academy, under Johann Peter von Langer, from 1813 to 1816*
- *early work in naturalistic style; later turned to religious painting*
- *important woman artist among the Nazarenes around Friedrich Overbeck*

Marie Ellenrieder was the first woman admitted to an art academy in Germany. She was no militant, however, but a pious woman who drew her self-confidence from her faith and who found an influential patron in the Baron von Wessenberg, a churchman from the southern German town of Constance. In 1813, she enrolled at the Munich Academy and by doing so helped pave the way for many other women to train there professionally – an opportunity that was unique in the whole of Europe in the first half of the nineteenth century.

Marie Ellenrieder was considered to be the most important German woman artist of her day. That she was later almost consigned to oblivion is not least due to her preferred genre of religious art. While her tender and charming images of the Madonna, angels and children at prayer enjoyed great popularity during her lifetime, now they are often felt to be overly sentimental. In contrast, her early realistic portraits appear fresh and original.

Ellenrieder's self-portrait of 1818 reveals a radiant twenty-seven-year-old, self-confidently and expectantly looking out into the world following the completion of her studies. At the time, she was especially keen on painting children's portraits, such as that of the five-year-old Thekla von Thurn-Valsassina. The way the girl has playfully curled her fingers around her necklace, the contented expression on her face and her short, rather tousled hair lend the girl a naturalness that is unusual in a German portrait of the Biedermeier period (c. 1815–48). Completed barely fifteen years later and representative of Ellenrieder's mature style, the painting *Maria Writing the Magnificat* appears to be the work of someone else. The unaf-

fected, true-to-life style has gone, as have the loose brushwork and the realistic depiction of light and her subject. This is a devotional picture in the tradition of the Italian Renaissance; it evokes a sense of piety that is far removed from its age. The enamel-like, smooth surface of the painting, its pure colours and harmonious lines lend it an idealized quality.

Influenced by her friend the Baron von Wessenberg, Ellenrieder became convinced that religious painting was her vocation. Her first large commission for an altarpiece enabled her, at the age of thirty-one, to undertake a study trip to Rome, where she soon met the Nazarenes, a circle of artists around the German painter Friedrich Overbeck. Their aim was to achieve a renewal of religious art in the spirit of Raphael, an ideal adopted by Ellenrieder, too. Although she was a more accomplished colourist than the other Nazarenes, many publications about the group's work mention her only in passing, if indeed at all.

Back in Germany, Ellenrieder concentrated wholly on religious subjects. She now executed portraits only in exceptional circumstances, such as when she received a commission from the Grand Duke of Baden, who appointed her his Court Painter in 1829. At the same time, her religious zeal required her to lead a life that was ascetic to the point of self-torment. Suffering from depression and growing deafness, Ellenrieder increasingly withdrew from society. Her creativity finally spent itself in variations on the Christ Child and the saints.

opposite
Marie Ellenrieder
Maria Writing the Magnificat, 1833
Oil on canvas, 64.8 x 46.2 cm
Kunsthalle, Karlsruhe

above
Marie Ellenrieder
Portrait of Thekla Maria Auguste von Thurn-Valsassina, 1818
Oil on canvas, 45 x 40 cm
Private collection, Schloss Bruchhausen, Sauerland

Rosa Bonheur

Among the many tourists who each year visit the former French royal residence at Fontainebleau, scarcely any know the name of Rosa Bonheur. Yet her home, the Château de By, lies on the edge of Fontainebleau's royal forest. During her lifetime, Bonheur was the most famous woman artist in France. Nowadays, the names of her contemporaries – Camille Corot, Théodore Rousseau or Charles-François Daubigny – more readily come to mind. After 1830, these men painted the unspoilt wooded countryside at nearby Barbizon and are now regarded as the forerunners of Impressionism. In contrast, Rosa Bonheur's painstaking realism is felt to belong to the conservative trends of nineteenth-century art that sank into obscurity with the rise of modernism.

Seemingly untouched, Rosa Bonheur's wide-brimmed hat hangs over the back of a chair in her Château de By studio, and sketches, brushes and palettes lie ready, with hunting trophies and stuffed animals in between – just where they were lying on 25 May 1899, when she died aged seventy-seven. The successful artist had bought the house in 1860 using her own funds. It was here, far from Parisian society, that Bonheur, her partner Nathalie Micas and her mother made a life that suited them. Nathalie's mother did the cooking and looked after the house while her eccentric daughter busied herself with inventions, such as a new type of braking system for the railway. Undisturbed, Bonheur devoted herself to painting – and her pets. She had already kept dogs and squirrels in Paris, but her country home became a veritable menagerie that included goats, parrots, horses, wild boars and even lions!

As a young girl, she had spared no effort to study animals wherever she had the chance. She drew in parks, in abattoirs and at the Paris horse market. To avoid unwanted gazes and comments from men, she slipped into men's clothes – with police permission! Comfortable trousers and an overall soon came to be her preferred attire in her studio, too, in place of the close-fitting, full-length dresses that were typically worn by women at the time. Even as a youngster she wore her hair short. In her own words, she was a stubborn, unruly child. Her father was an enthusiastic supporter of social reform, rejected all things conventional and never insisted that Rosa conform to female behavioural roles. Despite his meagre income as an art teacher, he made certain that his four children were able to realize their talent as

Rosa Bonheur
b. 16 March 1822
Bordeaux
d. 25 May 1899 Château
de By, Seine-et-Marne

- trained under her father, Raymond Bonheur, an art teacher and landscape painter
- ran an art school for young ladies from 1848 to 1859
- honorary president of the French Women Artists' Association
- biography, written by the American artist Anna Klumpke, and published in 1908

painters or sculptors. Rosa, the eldest, outshone them all. In 1853, she submitted *The Horse Fair* to the Paris Salon. This monumental canvas – almost two-and-a-half metres high and five metres wide – is dominated by the lively, powerful horses that trot and canter past the viewer's gaze in close procession. The atmosphere of the painting is intensified by the dramatic sky, which forms a striking contrast to the dark trees in the background. This brilliantly choreographed scene was acclaimed by the public of the day. The art dealer Ernest Gambart acquired it for his London gallery for the sum of 40,000 francs and had lithographs of it made, thus helping to make Bonheur known in England and, later, in the United States. In 1865, Bonheur became the first woman to be awarded the Grand Cross of the Legion of Honour, which was pinned to her breast by the Empress Eugénie herself as she uttered the words 'Genius knows no sex'.

Rosa Bonheur
The Horse Fair, 1853
Oil on canvas, 120 x 254.5 cm
National Gallery, London

Elizabeth Butler

The battle is over. Vanquished, wounded, collapsing from exhaustion and wearing blank expressions on their faces, the soldiers return from a battle that from the beginning had no prospect of success. Their British commanding officer had ordered his elite Light Brigade into action against a position held by Russian artillery. This battle during the Crimean War went down in history as the 'The Charge of the Light Brigade'. Although their deployment was pointless, the survivors were hailed as heroes.

When this battle was fought in 1854, Elizabeth Thompson was just eight years old. The painting was executed almost twenty-five years later, when the artist, born to British parents in French-speaking Switzerland in 1846, was already renowned for her battle scenes. Hers was an affluent, cultivated family and she, along with her sister Alice Meynell, profited from the educational opportunities that were then becoming available to women. Whereas Elizabeth attended the Female School of Art in the London borough of Kensington, where she studied classical art and the nude, Alice went on to become a famous poet and essayist who championed the rights of women.

Like many artists specializing in battle scenes, Elizabeth Butler had no personal experience of war, but she studied everything related to the military so thoroughly that her detailed paintings astonished her contemporaries. She questioned veterans, had authentic uniforms recreated and had both real soldiers and models pose for her in full uniform. She once bought a cornfield so that it could be trampled to make it look like a real battlefield.

With *Calling the Roll after an Engagement*, a scene from the Crimean War completed in 1874, the twenty-eight-year-old became famous almost overnight. Impressed by its forceful realism, so many visitors pressed round the painting at the Royal Academy that a policeman was put on duty to protect it. Some years later, the artist married Major, later General, Lord William Butler, a great admirer of her work, through whom she was able to observe military manoeuvres.

Much valued as a genre in the nineteenth century, battle scenes were the last remaining sphere of art into which women artists had not yet advanced. Warfare, after all, was the business of men. At most, women had to grapple with the consequences of war, either as mothers, wives and sisters mourning their dead or as nurses. With her work during the Crimean War, Florence Nightingale established modern nursing care for war casualties. Women play no part in Elizabeth Butler's paintings, however.

She was the only famous woman painter of battle scenes in the history of art. While her paintings do not conceal the horrors of war, they should not be misinterpreted as antiwar propaganda. Feminist scholars are at something of a loss when confronted with the artistic output of Elizabeth Butler, who died in 1933. To this day there is no comprehensive description of her work, although reproductions of it are still highly prized by collectors of militaria. The only major solo exhibition of her work so far was not organized by an art gallery, but by the National Army Museum in London.

Elizabeth Butler
b. 3 November 1846 Lausanne, Switzerland
d. 2 October 1933 Gormanston Castle, England

- *only renowned female painter of battle scenes in the history of art*
- *began to exhibit regularly after 1867*
- *her painting 'Calling the Roll after an Engagement' was purchased by Queen Victoria in 1874*
- *only just failed to be elected to the Royal Academy in 1879*

Elizabeth Butler
Balaclava, 1876
Oil on canvas, 76.2 x 41.9 cm
City Art Gallery, Manchester

Berthe Morisot

Berthe Morisot
b. 14 January 1841
Bourges
d. 2 March 1895 Passy
near Paris

- *trained under a number of painters, including Camille Corot*
- *exhibited her work regularly at the Paris Salon from 1864 to 1873*
- *in 1892 first solo exhibition, in the Galerie Boussod et Valadon, Paris*
- *most famous woman Impressionist besides Mary Cassatt*
- *executed paintings of domestic scenes, portraits and landscapes*

Lost in thought, a young mother regards her sleeping child in its cradle. With her left hand, she supports her chin – the classic melancholic pose – and with her right hand, she holds the veil protecting the child, whose small face can be seen only hazily through gossamer-thin tulle, shrouded in a glow of light and surrounded in delicate fabric. The lightly applied brushstrokes of the pink and blue highlights are clearly visible, as is the thinly applied white that allows the ochre ground to shine through. This intentionally sketchy technique lends the painting immediacy and spontaneity. Nonetheless, the work's balanced composition, with its generously sweeping lines and its restricted palette, imparts to it a timelessness that transcends momentary observation.

The long-established mother-and-child motif, especially popular during the nineteenth century, was given a new and unsentimental twist in this Impressionistic painting by Berthe Morisot. The young mother is Edma, the artist's sister. Berthe painted her countless times, either far advanced in pregnancy as she reclined on a sofa, catching butterflies, playing with her daughter or walking in the park. As youngsters and adolescents, Berthe and Edma, the elder by two years, were inseparable. Together they persuaded their wealthy parents to allow them to study art seriously under the guidance of a practitioner rather than give them the drawing and music lessons that were customary for young girls. Chaperoned by their mother, the girls set up their easels in the Louvre, where numerous other young painters gathered to copy the Old Masters. The renowned artist Camille Corot acquainted them with landscape painting. In 1864 the sisters successfully submitted their first paintings to the Salon. But then Edma met a naval officer, married him and stopped painting.

Berthe Morisot, however, remained true to art – and went on to become one of the most important female artists of her century. In 1868,

while copying in the Louvre, she met the painter Edouard Manet and the two of them developed a stimulating friendship. Morisot developed freer brushwork and she abandoned her muted palette for a brighter one. In turn, Manet was encouraged by her to paint outdoors. However, as an unmarried young woman from a better class of home, Morisot could not consider visiting the cafés and studios, where the Impressionists discussed their latest ideas. Her family thus invited painters such as Manet and Edgar Degas to its own salons and social gatherings.

In 1874 Berthe Morisot married Eugène Manet, the artist's younger brother. That same year, the first independent Impressionist exhibition caused a sensation among the art lovers of Paris. Morisot showed nine paintings in it – including *The Cradle* – despite the fact that Manet had advised her against doing so. The conservative art critics reacted maliciously and scornfully to the works of the Impressionists, describing them as unfinished sketches and amateurish smears of paint.

Morisot, however, was convinced of this new style of unacademic painting and henceforth belonged to the core group of Impressionist painters alongside Degas, Claude Monet and Auguste Renoir. Her importance lies not least in the fact that she applied an Impressionistic technique to her very own themes of the domestic setting and the everyday life of women from the upper middle classes.

Berthe Morisot
The Cradle, 1872
Oil on canvas, 46 x 56 cm
Musée d'Orsay, Paris

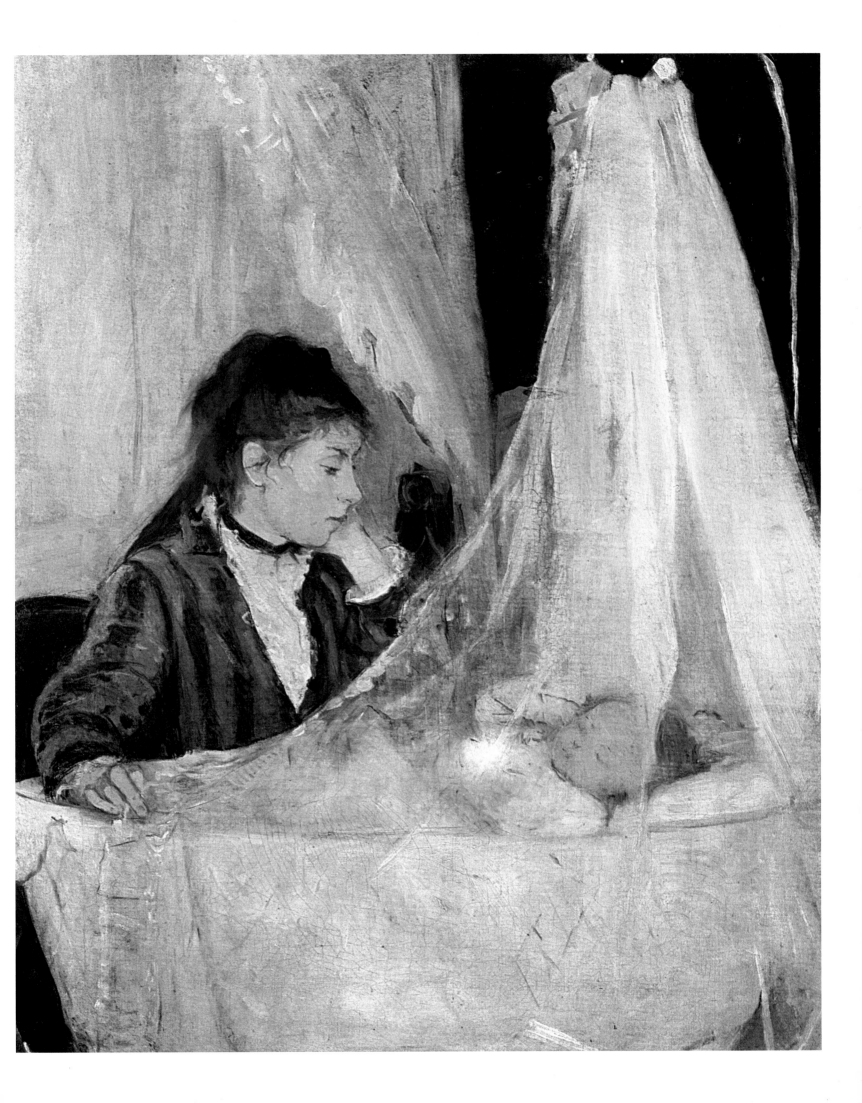

Mary Cassatt

MARY CASSATT
b. 22 May 1844 Pitts-
burgh, Pennsylvania
d. 14 June 1926 Mesnil-
Beaufresne

- *began to exhibit work at Impressionist shows in Paris after 1879*
- *played a major role in making Impressionism known in the United States*
- *was one f the most important American artists of her time*
- *also left behind a significant body of graphic work*
- *awarded the Cross of the Legion of Honour in 1904*

In the autumn of 1875, the thirty-one-year-old American artist Mary Cassatt rented a studio in the Parisian district of Montmartre. The daughter of a wealthy banker, she had already studied at Philadelphia's Academy of Fine Arts and had set off for Europe, where she wanted to continue with art lessons in the leading art centres of the day, Paris and Rome. As was called for by propriety, a female friend or her mother always accompanied her. For many years she travelled throughout Italy, the Netherlands, Spain and France, copying Old Masters and working under different artists. She first exhibited her work at the Paris Salon in 1868.

Increasingly, however, she began to regard the majority of the paintings on show there as unsatisfactory and bland. Year by year, artists such as Paul Cézanne, Edgar Degas or Claude Monet had their paintings rejected by the Salon's conservative judges. The two paintings submitted by Mary Cassatt in 1877 were also declined. At Degas's suggestion, Cassatt then joined the Impressionists and at their next show exhibited twelve works, among them her 'study' At the Opera. With its generous treatment of colour, this painting was probably too sketchily rendered even by Impressionist standards to be considered adequate. Its theme is a scene from contemporary city life, a favourite subject among the Impressionists. While they were a source of motifs for many male artists, the nightclubs and dancehalls frequented by the demimonde were off limits to a 'respectable' woman like Cassatt, who was therefore obliged to observe the activities of the fashionable bourgeoisie at the Paris Opera.

Sitting in her box, a young woman in a high-necked dress closely follows the events on stage through an opera glass. What she sees remains hidden. The viewer, however, is witness to a gentleman in another box observing the woman through his own opera glass as he leans over the balustrade. Cassatt captures the scene skilfully, lending it a charged atmosphere. The woman is actively engaged in observing while being observed herself. Around this time, a woman could never feel she was *not* under observation and it was anything but a matter of course for a woman to meet the world around her with an open, self-confident gaze. Eva Gonzalès, a pupil of Edouard Manet, also explored this theme around 1874. In her painting of a couple in their box at the theatre, the viewer shares in the glances of the artist's subjects. The young woman at the centre of the painting appears to be so close as to give the impression that the viewer himself is observing her through his opera glass.

Images of public life are rare in Cassatt's work. Like her friend Berthe Morisot, she recorded the everyday life of bourgeois women, which was centred on the home. She took a particular interest in mother-and-child scenes, in which she lends her female subjects the dignity of Madonnas. These paintings were extremely popular in France and America and, partly at the insistence of her art dealers, Cassatt produced more and more variations on the theme from the 1880s onwards.

above
Eva Gonzalès
A Box at the Théâtre des Italiens,
1874. Oil on canvas, 98 x 130 cm
Musée d'Orsay, Paris

opposite
Mary Cassatt
At the Opera, 1879/80
Oil on canvas, 81 x 66 cm
Museum of Fine Arts, Boston

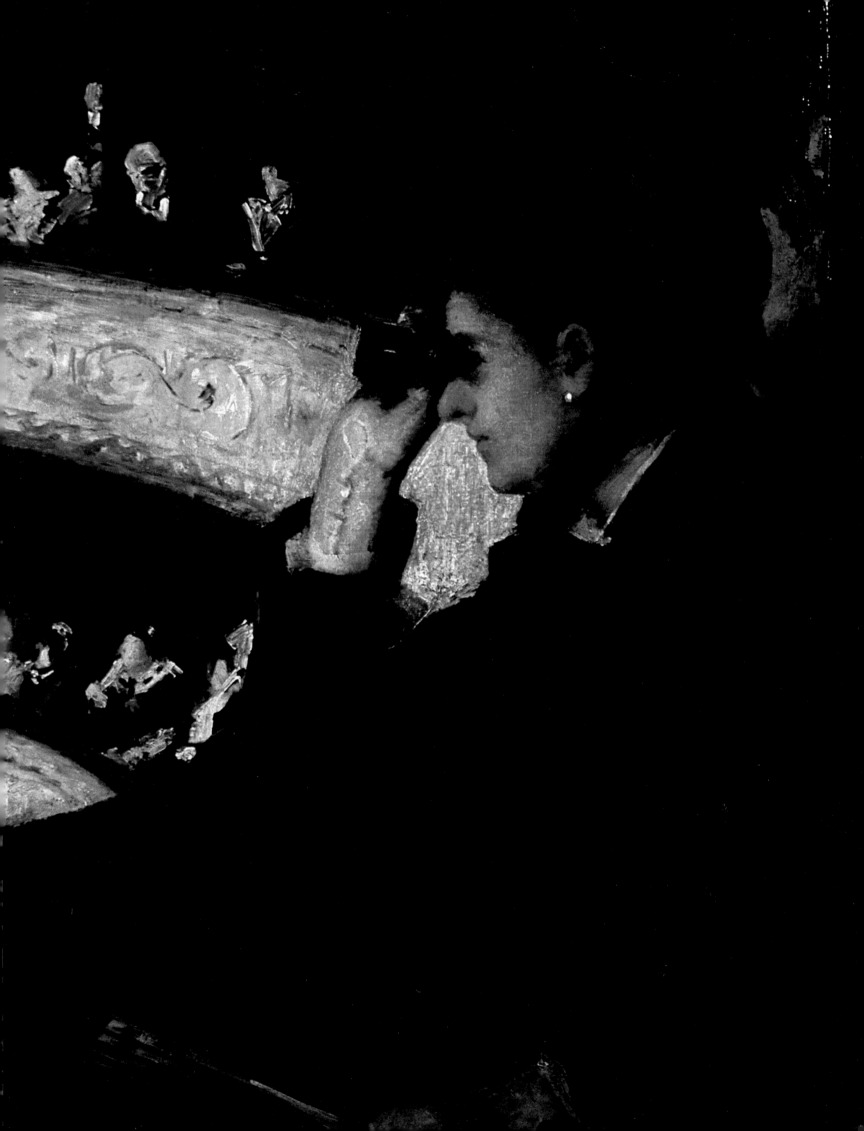

Camille Claudel

Camille Claudel's life is the stuff of novels and films, and exhibitions of her work now attract large numbers of visitors. Above all, it was the story of her unrequited love for Auguste Rodin that assured the sculptor of widespread attention. Yet, for all they share with Rodin's work, her own pieces possess power and originality. Her sculptures express vital experiences, such as love, desire, death and old age, and do so with great directness and vigour.

Camille Claudel was born the daughter of a civil servant in 1864 in the French province of Champagne. She discovered her delight in modelling clay while still a child. As a spirited young woman, she insisted on fulfilling her wish to be trained as an artist when her family moved to Paris in 1881. With the support of the sculptor Alfred Boucher, she enrolled at the renowned Académie Colarossi and exhibited some early pieces at the Salon. When she was nineteen, she met the sculptor Auguste Rodin, a man more than twice her age. Under his guidance, she fashioned portrait busts and female nudes, worked in marble, modelled for him and was employed in his workshop. A passionate love affair soon developed from their close collaboration, but from the start it was fraught with conflict and jealousies. It was an unequal relationship: for a man like Rodin, an illicit affair presented no obstacles to his career, but for a young woman from a good family, it meant a break with all the social norms. At one point, Claudel forced a promise of marriage out of Rodin, which he never kept. In 1888 Claudel moved into her own studio flat and Rodin rented a nearby house for use as a studio and meeting place for them both.

The sculpture *Sakountala* dates from this time. It was suggested to her by a piece of Indian literature describing the reunion of two long-separated lovers. In a highly personal interpretation, Claudel uses an unconventional pose to express the old theme of two lovers: the man kneels before his lover, who sinks into his arms, her eyes closed as she abandons herself utterly to her feelings. Everything is free-flowing expression of emotion; the sculpture's surface appears soft and alive, and pulsates with life. In comparison to it, Rodin's *Kiss*, created only a short time before, appears to be more conventional in its use of form and more restrained in its emotional expression.

When the artist had the opportunity seventeen years later to execute *Sakountala* in marble, her halcyon days with Rodin had long since vanished. Even after separating from him, she was unable to rid herself of her reputation as his protégée. Artistically, too, the sculptor made a greater effort to distance herself from him by turning to new subjects and making small-scale scenes, such as with *The Gossips* or the onyx *Wave* with its group of women bathers. The long years spent in search of recognition and struggling to make a living took their toll, however. Claudel's creative power failed her, her frame of mind deteriorated and she believed that Rodin, and everyone else, was persecuting her. Visitors described how she was increasingly failing to look after herself and how, in fits of despair, she would destroy her work. Only a few days after her father's death, her brother, the author Paul Claudel, had her admitted to an asylum in 1913. In the years that followed, she tried in vain to persuade her family to allow her to return to normal life. Camille Claudel died on 19 October 1943 after spending thirty years in asylums. Today a large part of her work is on display at the Musée Rodin in Paris – just as Rodin had intended in 1914.

Camille Claudel
b. 8 December 1864
Fère-en-Tardenois, Aisne
d. 19 October 1943 Montdevergues near Avignon

- *important sculptor in the group around Rodin*
- *began exhibiting her work at the Paris Salon in 1882*
- *shared a studio with sculptor Jessie Lipscomb*
- *was active for about 20 years*

Camille Claudel
Sakountala or *L'Abandon*, 1905
Marble
Musée Rodin, Paris

Suzanne Valadon

Suzanne Valadon
b. 23 September 1865
Bessines-sur-Gartempe,
Haute Vienne, France
d. 7 April 1938 Paris

- Valadon achieved fame
  mainly through her
  unconventional paintings
  of women and nudes
- first solo exhibition in
  1911, at the Galerie
  Clovis Sagot, later at
  Galerie Berthe Weill,
  among others
- became a member of the
  'Modern Women Artists'
  Association' in 1933
- retrospective held in
  1932 at the Galerie
  Georges Petit, Paris

Suzanne Valadon can be seen in many paintings from the end of the nineteenth century, having sat for the Symbolist painter Pierre Puvis de Chavannes, the Impressionist Pierre-Auguste Renoir, for Henri de Toulouse-Lautrec and academic painters. Even as an adolescent, this illegitimate daughter of a seamstress had to support herself in various jobs; among other things, she worked as a shop assistant, a waitress and a circus acrobat in Montmartre. With her striking beauty and uninhibited nature, Marie-Clementine Valadon (she later adopted the name Suzanne) became a well-known model and – like many women in this situation – was a lover to the artists who painted her. Bourgeois notions of morality and decency were meaningless to Valadon, a woman from the lower social orders. When, aged eighteen, she gave birth to her son, Maurice Utrillo, she probably was none too sure herself who his father was. The boy was raised by his grandmother while his mother worked as a model. Utrillo later achieved fame as a painter of Parisian street scenes.

Suzanne Valadon never attended art school or trained under a painter. What she did, however, was carefully observe the artists for whom she sat and took note of how they chose their colours, conceived their compositions and sketched their lines. Indeed Valadon drew 'like a maniac' (her own words), choosing as her subjects her son, her elderly mother and local prostitutes. She particularly enjoyed painting female nudes, and gave them bold, expressive outlines. Impressed by her rare talent, Edgar Degas was the first to purchase her drawings and became a close friend of the artist.

She plucked up the courage to try her hand at oil painting only in the second half of her life. The painting *Adam and Eve* dates from 1909, the year Valadon, now over forty, left her wealthy husband to live with a man twenty-one years her junior, André Utter. Posing as Adam for her, he was her first male nude. Like Paul Gauguin, Valadon stylizes the bodies through her bold use of black contours. Combining the two figures harmoniously, she clearly contrasts Adam's angular form with Eve's soft curves. Unlike earlier paintings on the theme, the biblical sinner Eve is not presented as the temptress here; it is more the case that Adam helps her to pick the irresistible fruit while they embrace each other tenderly. Before she was able to exhibit the painting, Valadon had to conceal Adam's groin with vine leaves.

In 1914, she married the young painter Utter. Henceforth they and her alcoholic son formed an 'accursed trinity', as they described themselves, a crisis-ridden household beyond all bourgeois conventions. At times their paintings sold well and they splashed out with their earnings; at other times they lived in abject poverty. Valadon held to her distinctive and personal style right until the end of her life, despite the rise of such new artistic trends as Cubism and abstract painting. When Valadon died, aged seventy-three, she was recognized in France and beyond as one of the foremost female artists of her generation.

Suzanne Valadon
Adam and Eve, 1909
Oil on canvas, 162 x 131 cm
Musée National d'Art Moderne,
Centre Georges Pompidou, Paris

The Twentieth Century

before 1945

Gwen John

Paula Modersohn-Becker

Gabriele Münter

Natalia Goncharova

Sonia Delaunay-Terk

Hannah Höch

Käthe Kollwitz

Tamara de Lempicka

Georgia O'Keeffe

Frida Kahlo

Meret Oppenheim

orges Braque   Umberto Boccioni   Erich Heckel   Amedeo Modigliani   Max Beckmann   Kurt Schwitters   Otto Dix   George Grosz   René Magritte   Salvador Dalí

ever before had there been so many new impulses, such a wealth of styles and so many conflicting trends as in the art of the twentieth century. In an age distinguished by the ever faster exchange of information, improved travel opportunities and international contact, new developments in art spread with greater speed than ever before – and were just as soon superseded by other developments. The art of the first half of the century is known as early modernism, a term that describes no particular style, but rather a basic attitude towards art that is characterized by a rejection of tradition. Quality was no longer judged using criteria such as the accurate portrayal of the body and its proportions, the ability to reproduce colour and light faithfully or to draw 'properly'. Instead, artistic expression was to be both credible and powerful. The artist and his or her work became the measure of all things.

With their highly stylized, dreamy imaginings, Symbolism and Art Nouveau shaped the art of the turn of the century; at the same time, however, Impressionism, originating in France, came to be regarded internationally as the root of modern art. In protest against the art establishment and its academic practices, artists such

as the the Austrian Jugendstil painter Gustav Klimt and the German Impressionist Max Liebermann founded the 'Sezessionen'; these were independent artists' associations in which new ideas could be exchanged freely. Yet they, too, soon turned out to be conservative bastions compared with the exponents of the latest trends, such as Expressionism, a European counter-movement to Impressionism, with its delicate palette and light-filled canvases. Practitioners of the new style included the 'Fauves', artists around Henri Matisse in Paris, and artists in Dresden known as 'Die Brücke' (The Bridge), among them Ernst Ludwig Kirchner and Erich Heckel, but also the north German individualist Emil Nolde and the Viennese Expressionists Egon Schiele and Oskar Kokoschka. Reproducing an impression of what they saw concerned them less than giving powerful expression to their emotions, something they strove to achieve through greater intensity of colour and the use of simplified forms – taking their cues from the 'Post-Impressionists' Vincent van Gogh, Paul Gauguin and Paul Cézanne. In Munich, artists such as Franz Marc, Wassily Kandinsky and Gabriele Münter established the 'Blaue Reiter' (Blue Rider) group. Using glowing

above left
Pablo Picasso
Les Demoiselles d'Avignon,
1907
Oil on canvas, 243.9 x 233.7 cm
The Museum of Modern Art,
New York

above centre
Wassily Kandinsky
Composition VII, 1913
Oil on canvas, 200 x 300 cm
Tretyakov State Gallery,
Moscow

above right
Kasimir Malevich
Black Square, 1914-15
Oil on canvas, 79.5 x 79.5 cm
Tretyakov State Gallery,
Moscow

colours, they created pictures that became increasingly detached from the natural world, a development that would lead Kandinsky to produce his first abstract works, his series of Improvisations of 1910, which were only remotely reminiscent of landscapes or human figures.

In their search for an original and vigorous mode of expression, many artists found inspiration in the folk art of their own countries and in the 'primitive' art of Africa or Oceania. For Pablo Picasso, too, who executed the melancholy paintings of his so-called Blue and Rose Periods in Paris after 1901, African masks and sculpture were an important source of inspiration, as seen in his 1907 picture Les Demoiselles d'Avignon, a key work of modern art. In it, he lent his female nudes simplified, angular forms and mask-like, distorted features. This painting marks the beginning of Cubism, which Picasso created in close association with the Frenchman Georges Braque, in whose work objects are reduced to their basic shapes. In a parallel development in Italy, artists such as Giacomo Balla and Umberto Boccioni developed Futurism after 1910. Moreover, the depiction of speed and motion was central to their work.

Before the First World War, a multifarious avant-garde movement also developed in Russia. It united Western stylistic trends and elements of Russian folk art, as exemplified by the primitivism and 'Cubo-Futurist' style of Natalia Goncharova and Mikhail Larionov. Also Russian, Kasimir Malevich made a crucial contribution to the emergence of abstract art with his radically simplified and purely geometric paintings, such as Black Square, for which he coined the term 'Suprematism'. Following the 1917 October Revolution, abstract avant-garde art became emblematic of the renewal of Russian society. Constructivists like El Lissitzky, Alexander Rodchenko or Vladimir Tatlin applied abstract-geometric forms to the fields of industry, technology, architecture and design. In the Netherlands, the Constructivist painters and architects around Theo van Doesburg and Piet Mondrian established De Stijl. In Weimar, the German architect Walter Gropius founded the Bauhaus school of art and design in 1919. With

people like Lyonel Feininger or Paul Klee on its staff, it became one of the most famous and influential art schools of the twentieth century.

Naturalistic and figurative trends in art gained fresh impetus in the 1920s. Europe's social order had been shaken to its foundations by the First World War, an occurrence that also had repercussions for the art world. Still during the war, in 1916, the Dada movement crystallized in Zurich. Artists such as Marcel Duchamp, George Grosz, Man Ray and Kurt Schwitters soon became its representatives in Cologne, Berlin, New York and Paris. In a nihilistic frenzy, these artists attacked traditional artistic and moral values in their scathing satires, collages, nonsense poems and ready-made objects. In 1920s Paris, Dadaists, such as the sculptor Hans Arp or the painter Max Ernst, joined the Surrealists around the writer André Breton. Inspired by Sigmund Freud's psychoanalytical theories, they made the subconscious the basis of their creative work. In the surrealistic fantasies of such artists as Salvador Dalí, René Magritte or Giorgio de Chirico, eroticism and sexuality play an important role, and their paintings often have a dream-like quality.

The German artists associated with 'Neue Sachlichkeit' (New Objectivity), most notably Otto Dix, instead observed the social and political situation around them. American Precisionists took as their subject urban and industrial America, while the Regionalists were concerned with painting Midwestern scenes. In the work of Edward Hopper, for instance, the loneliness of city life is the central theme.

In Germany under the Nazis after 1933 and under the communist regime of the Soviet Union, state policy dictated the direction art took, using it for propaganda purposes, thus making it impossible for art to develop freely. German Jewish artists fled Germany if they could; German opposition artists could opt for 'inner emigration', a withdrawal into private life. Many, however, left for the United States, where they took up teaching posts in art colleges and influenced a new generation of American artists. Following the Second World War, Europe was no longer to be the centre of the art world, but instead the United States.

The Russian Avant-garde

In no other modern artistic movement has the participation of women been such a matter of course and so influential as in the avant-garde of pre-revolutionary Russia. That said, these 'Amazons of the avant-garde', as the contemporary poet Benedikt Livsic described them, by no means formed a uniform group; they represented neither the same style nor the same social or political aims. Yet they were active in the same place at the same time and knew each other, and also seem to have had good working relations with their male counterparts. Creative partnerships developed between Natalia Goncharova and Mikhail Larionov, Varvara Stepanova and Alexander Rodchenko, Nadezhda Udaltsova and Alexander Drevin as well as between Olga Rosanova and the poet Alexei Kruchenykh.

Russia's avant-garde women artists came from comfortable, and often even aristocratic, families, which enabled them to study. Especially at the start of their careers, their social status gave them self-confidence when dealing with their male peers, who frequently came from more humble backgrounds. These women also benefited from the fact that in 1871 the St Petersburg and Moscow art academies had begun to admit female art students, which meant that a first generation of professional women artists had already made a name for itself. The fair degree of

Lyubov Popova, *Painterly Architectonics*, 1917
Oil on canvas, 107 x 88 cm
Krasnodar Regional Art Museum, Krasnodar

freedom enjoyed by these avant-garde women artists in their careers and 'lifestyle' was exceptional for Russian society at the time, however. The majority of the population lived in abject poverty in rural areas under a patriarchal system; in the country's urban centres, too, women did not enjoy equality. Women artists did benefit from the spirit of optimism that existed between 1910 and 1925 among intellectuals, however.

The artist Alexandra Exter was a conduit for the exchange of ideas between Western Europe and Russia's art centres. Aged twenty-five, she travelled to Paris and other European cities and made contact with Pablo Picasso, Guillaume Apollinaire and Ardengo Soffici, introducing her compatriots to French Cubism and Italian Futurism.

From Cubist townscapes she progressed to abstract colour compositions, which she also translated into designs for stage sets. Also in Paris, Lyubov Popova and Nadezhda Udaltsova studied Cubist painting and explored its possibilities. In co-operation with Kasimir Malevich, Popova later turned to the geometric, abstract realm of Suprematism and created works such as *Painterly Architectonics*, 1917, which reveals her use of powerfully dynamic forms. With painting on canvas held to be outdated during the period of change in society that followed the October Revolution in 1917, Popova soon applied her new formal idiom to commercial art. Similarly, other women artists, such as Olga Rosanova or Varvara Stepanova, devoted themselves to the design of fabrics, stage scenery, posters and books. Natalia Goncharova, on the other hand, did not return to Russia after the Revolution and Alexandra Exter also went into exile in 1924, when the contours of Stalin's repressive policies began to emerge.

Events in History: The Twentieth Century before 1945

1905
Albert Einstein publishes his *Special Theory of Relativity*.

1914
Beginning of the First World War, which lasts until 1918.

1917
The October Revolution in Russia leads to the fall of the tsars.

1918
Proclamation of the Weimar Republic. Foundation of the 'Bauhaus'. Beginning of prohibition in the United States.

1927
Charles Lindbergh flies non-stop across the Atlantic.

1929
'Black Friday': collapse of the New York stock market. Foundation of the Museum of Modern Art in New York.

1933
Hitler becomes 'Reichskanzler' – Chancellor of the German Reich. Franklin D. Roosevelt becomes president of the US and initiates New Deal Program to end the Depression.

1939
The Second World War begins with Germany's invasion of Poland.

1941
German invasion of the Soviet Union. Japan enters the war at Pearl Harbor.

1945
Capitulation of Germany. American atom bombs dropped on Hiroshima and Nagasaki. Foundation of the UN.

Gwen John

In her 1929 essay 'A Room of One's Own', Virginia Woolf describes how little appreciated it was in her day that women needed a space of their own – and just how much creative pursuits and intellectual independence depended on one. For the women artists, too, who went to Paris around the turn of the century, a small room in a boarding house or a modest and furnished studio flat often represented their very own refuge, whose peace and quiet they enjoyed and needed. No one captured this in painting more skilfully than Gwen John, who was twenty-seven when, in 1903, she moved from London to Paris, where she settled permanently.

In spring 1907, she moved to an attic room at number 87, Rue du Cherche-Midi. She painted it on several occasions, both with the window open and showing a view of the tenement opposite and closed, the room quiet, the curtains drawn. A wicker chair with an item of clothing hanging over it, a white parasol and a narrow table are reminders of the woman who lives here, the woman who is absent yet present. Despite its unassuming, ordinary theme, the painting possesses great artistic power. It has a rough surface and its few warm colours harmonize with each other. The artist has arranged her objects in a balanced way across her canvas as in an abstract-geometrical composition: the sloping edge of the pitch of the roof, the lines of the parasol and chair going in the opposite direction, the bright rectangle of the window and the brown floor with its six-sided tiles.

John's contemporaries, Amedeo Modigliani and Giorgio Morandi, with their pared-down still lifes, created an equally meditative and timeless atmosphere in their paintings. Above all, Gwen John was concerned with her 'interior life' (as she herself called it), with expressing her feelings. All her work is characterized by an unusual severity of form and economy of means. She was persistent in executing varia-

tions on her preferred subjects: slender female figures, serious nuns, women reading, simple still lifes and deserted interiors – men scarcely feature in her work.

To earn a living, John sat for artists, including Auguste Rodin, whose lover she became – just as the sculptor Camille Claudel had done years before her. This unequal partnership also led John into a personal crisis. For almost ten years, she pestered the much older Rodin with hundreds of letters, and she moved into the suburb of Meudon where he lived, to find comfort in Roman Catholicism. Although she led a secluded life, John closely followed what was happening in the Paris art world. She met Pablo Picasso and Georges Braque, was an admirer of Paul Cézanne and also showed her work at exhibitions in Europe and America. Success meant little to her, however. In 1910, the American collector John Quinn began to buy and promote her paintings, thus enabling her to make a living.

During her lifetime, Gwen John was mainly known as the sister of the successful painter Augustus John, but today her work is represented in major collections of modern art – from New York's Metropolitan Museum of Art to the Tate Gallery in London.

Gwen John
b. 22 June 1876
Haverfordwest, Wales
d. 18 September 1939
Dieppe, France

- *trained at the Slade School of Art in London and under James McNeill Whistler in Paris*
- *won the Melville Nettleship Prize as a student*
- *exhibited her work at the 1913 'Armory Show' in New York*
- *ranks among the most important British artists of the 20th century*

Gwen John
Corner of the Artist's Room, 1907-09
Oil on canvas, 31.8 x 26.7 cm
Sheffield City Art Galleries, Sheffield

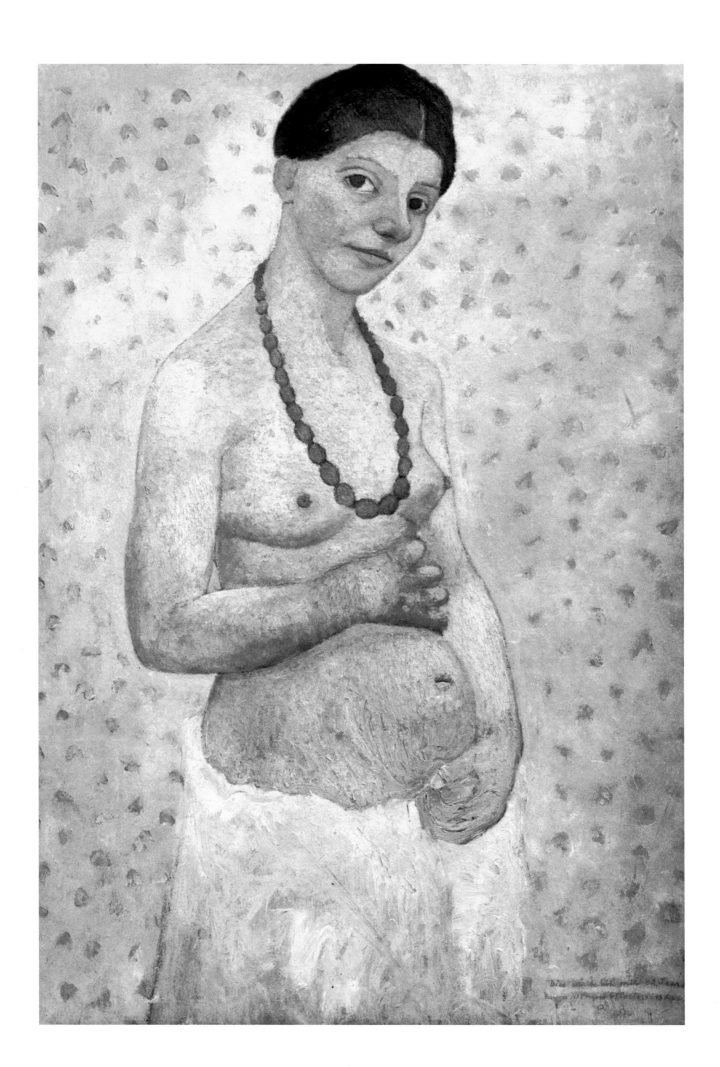

Paula Modersohn-Becker

At the turn of last century, Worpswede was a remote village in the flat countryside near the German city of Bremen. It was home to simple peasants and peat-cutters; fields, solitary birch trees and moors characterized the empty landscape. Around 1895, a group of young artists had settled there to allow them to paint nature in its simplicity and purity, far removed from the world of academic painting. They were joined in 1898 by twenty-two-year-old Paula Becker, who had finished studying at the college run by the Berlin School of Art for Women. Three years later she married the landscape painter Otto Modersohn, a member of the Worpswede group. The rising sculptor Clara Westhoff, who would later marry the German poet Rainer Maria Rilke, became her close friend.

Away from the confines of the Worpswede artists' colony, Becker discovered a different world in Paris, where, on several visits after 1900, she spent some months attending classes at the Académie Colarossi and the Ecole des Beaux-Arts. Paris offered her a wealth of inspiration, either in Paul Gauguin's dreamy South Sea paintings, Paul Cézanne's still lifes with their concern for underlying structure or the art of ancient Greece, Rome and Egypt, which she saw in the Louvre – it all influenced her style.

Increasingly, Modersohn-Becker strove to achieve greatness and simplicity in her painting. She reduced her palette, combined her forms into large areas and emphasized shape through her use of broad, almost crude, dark outlines. Many artists at the beginning of the twentieth century consciously turned away from the refined fin-de-siècle culture they regarded as decadent and were absorbed in a search for the simple, the original, the primitive even.

Paula Modersohn-Becker found her themes and models in the simple countrywomen, children and impoverished widows of Worpswede. Women, in fact, are the main theme of her work, and the artist lent them dignity and monumentality – attractive, erotic or graceful they are not! Likewise, the children in her paintings are not adorable little things; instead, they look out at us seriously and strangely. This complete rejection of the prevailing ideals of beauty was sharply criticized by her contemporaries and was regarded as amateurism or misinterpreted as a 'cult of the ugly'. Yet Modersohn-Becker was concerned with finding timeless and direct forms of expression and with creating symbols of human existence. In her numerous self-portraits, too, she eschewed realism, stylizing her appearance in reduced, expressive form. Lacking the attributes of her profession, these vivid, introspective images do not show her as a painter, but as a woman. On several occasions, she painted nude portraits of herself, which was highly unusual for a woman then. She appears pensive in the self-portrait she painted on her sixth wedding anniversary. Stripped to the waist, she has placed her hands across her front and stands facing the viewer. Her stomach is rounded and suggests pregnancy. Both privately and artistically, Modersohn-Becker had addressed the issue of motherhood, although she was not pregnant at the time. Shortly after giving birth to her first child the following year (1907), the artist died from an obstructed artery. She was only thirty-one.

In the course of her short life, Modersohn-Becker produced around 750 paintings, 1,000 drawings and a dozen prints. Like Van Gogh, she died too young to see the success of her art. During her lifetime, she sold no more than two or three paintings, yet she now ranks as an important modernist artist – and her fame surpasses that of her Worpswede colleagues, who once enjoyed greater success.

Paula Modersohn-Becker
b. 8 February 1876
Dresden
d. 21 November 1907
Worpswede

- *first art lessons in London in 1892*
- *influenced by the avant-garde in Paris and ancient Egyptian art*
- *during her lifetime, her work was exhibited only twice in Bremen's Art Gallery*
- *her paintings were denounced as 'degenerate' by the Nazis*

Paula-Modersohn-Becker
Self-portrait on 6th Wedding Anniversary, 1906
Oil on cardboard, 101.8 x 70.2 cm
Paula-Becker-Modersohn-Haus, Bremen

Gabriele Münter

Clouds scud across the sky, the trees bend in the wind. In Gabriele Münter's painting, the movement of the storm across the countryside seems to be taken up even by the mountain-tops, roofs and garden walls. Their lines sweep rhythmically across the canvas, but despite its overall impression of dynamism, the composition gives an impression of stability, each of its parts immovable. Black contours lend them solidity and a clear structure – and form the framework of the composition. The well-defined blue, red, ochre and green planes of colour clash force-fully. In this painting, Münter expressed her impressions of the countryside on a stormy day that she experienced in 1910 in the Alpine foothills near Murnau. She dispenses with everything that is insignifi-cant, whether inconvenient detail or naturalistic nuances of colour, and thus heightens the impression made by the paint-ing. Wind and Weather is charac-teristic of Münter's style between 1908 and 1910, an extremely productive and decisive phase in her development as an artist.

At the time, she was working closely with Wassily Kandinsky whom she had met in 1902 on enrolling at his newly opened Phalanx School of Art in Munich. The Russian artist was just embarking on his own career and experi-menting with Impressionistic open-air painting. He had a long way to go before he made the transition to abstraction. After an extended period of travel, in 1908 they settled – unmar-ried – in the small town of Murnau, where Münter bought a house. Their friend, the artist Alexei Jawlensky, told them about the latest Parisian trends in art, especially Henri Matisse's use of vibrant, expressive colour. Jawlensky's glamorous partner, Marianne von Werefkin, animated their discussions with her ideas about the creation of new and 'true' art. These were artists in excited mood. Driven by creative rivalry, Münter and Kandinsky used brilliant colours in their landscapes that increasingly became detached from the natural world, a development that would lead Kandinsky to abstract art around 1910. For Münter, however, a response to the world she saw around her remained essential. A diary entry from 1911 formulates her aims as an artist: '…from reproducing nature… – to feeling the essence – to abstracting – to rendering the essence'.

With Franz Marc and others, Kandinsky and Münter formed the 'Blaue Reiter' (Blue Rider), a short-lived but highly influential artists' association whose grandiose plans were wrecked by the outbreak of the First World War. As a Russian citizen, Kandinsky had to return home in 1914. Although tension was growing in their relationship, Münter still expected him to return, relying on a promise of marriage he had made to her. After 1915, she waited for him in neutral Sweden. Kandinsky, however, married a young Russian woman in Moscow in 1917. On hearing about their marriage only much later, Münter fell into a severe depression and was unable to work. She resumed painting only much later at the insistence of her future part-ner, the scholar Johannes Eichner. In 1957, she donated the paintings by Kandinsky that had been left with her, and some of her own work, to the Lenbachhaus in Munich. Her home in Murnau is now a museum.

Gabriele Münter
b. 19 February 1877 Berlin
d. 19 May 1962 Murnau

- *received first art training in Düsseldorf under Ernst Bosch and Willy Platz*
- *inspired by Bavarian folk art, she also produced panels of 'verre églomisé'*
- *her colourful landscapes and still lifes make her one of the most significant female Expressionist painters*
- *first biography written by her husband, Johannes Eichner*

left
Gabriele Münter
Portrait of Marianne von Werefkin, 1909
Oil on cardboard, 81 x 55 cm
Städtische Gallerie im Lenbachhaus, Munich

above
Gabriele Münter
Wind and Weather, 1910
Oil on cardboard, 50 x 65 cm
Sprengel Museum, Hanover

Natalia Goncharova

Natalia Goncharova was thirty-two years old when a major retrospective of her work was held in Moscow, in 1913. Comprising more than seven hundred items, the exhibition was a huge success with the public – even if the critics remained sharply divided over it. Goncharova was at the height of her career as a member of the Russian avant-garde. She had already exhibited her work in western Europe: in Paris in 1907, in Munich with the 'Blaue Reiter' (Blue Rider) in 1912 and in Berlin at Herwarth Walden's celebrated 'First German Salon d'Automne' in 1913 – alongside the work of such artists as Wassily Kandinsky, Gabriele Münter and Paul Klee.

Goncharova's life and work were shaped by two extremes: her Russian origins and Western-influenced modernism. She was born into the educated and liberal aristocracy and grew up on her family's country estates. Around 1900, she met the painter and designer Mikhail Larionov at the Moscow School of Painting, Sculpture and Architecture, and the two of them began a lifelong love affair and working relationship. Both were key figures in Moscow's avant-garde, who shocked the bourgeoisie with their unconventional behaviour. They exhibited with the 'Knave of Diamonds' group and held heated debates about the latest avant-garde trends in Paris.

Goncharova immediately embraced ideas from the West and combined them with Russian traditions. She first painted in an Impressionistic style, but soon discovered the work of Paul Gauguin and Paul Cézanne. From her examination of Cubism, she eventually developed a Neo-primitive style characterized by block-like forms, strong colours and motifs taken from peasant life. Her models were Russian peasant art, with its crude woodcuts and decorative patterns, as well as Byzantine icon paintings.

Her 1913 *Portrait of Larionov* is in the Rayonist style and thus marks a new phase in her development as an artist. Rayonism was based on a theory that Larionov expounded in the Rayonist manifesto of the same year and which Goncharova signed. It held that all objects emit rays that are intercepted by other objects nearby. The task of artists was to make these rays visible in their paintings. Goncharova's portrait of Larionov reveals a typically fragmented use of colour, especially around the edges. His flat-looking face appears to have been unfolded to reveal various facets. There are obvious similarities both with Cubism and the way it deconstructs its subjects, as seen in the work of Pablo Picasso and Georges Braque, and the dynamic rhythms of Italian Futurism – even if Rayonism was intended by Goncharova and Larionov to be an original Russian avant-garde style.

Goncharova soon took up new challenges, however. The renowned impresario Sergei Diaghilev, the founder of the Ballets Russes in Paris, invited her to design sets for his production of *The Golden Cockerel* after the opera by Nikolai Rimsky-Korsakov. From then on, the theatre became the focus of her work as an artist. For the music of Claude Debussy and Stravinsky, she designed colourful, ultra-modern costumes and sets influenced by Eastern folklore, and accompanied the Ballets Russes on tours through France, Italy and Spain. Natalia Goncharova returned to Russia only once more, in 1915, eventually becoming a French citizen. In 1962 – two years before her companion, Larionov – she died in Paris.

Natalia Goncharova
b. 21 June 1881 Nega-
yevo, Russia
d. 17 October 1962
Paris

- *trained as a sculptor and painter at Moscow School of Art from 1898 to 1910*
- *main female exponent of the Russian avant-garde*
- *also executed graphic work*
- *major retrospective held in 1963 at the Musée d'Art Moderne in Paris*

Natalia Goncharova
Portrait of Larionov, 1913
Oil on canvas, 105 x 78 cm
Museum Ludwig, Cologne

Sonia Delaunay-Terk

Colour is what energizes the work of Sonia Delaunay-Terk, a woman with an instinctive feel for colour combinations, which she realized not only in paintings, but also in fabric, clothing and interior decoration. For her, the boundary between art and crafts was a fluid one. Little is known about the first twenty years of her life other than that she was born Sarah Stern in the Ukrainian town of Gradizhsk and that, when still a small child, she was sent away to St Petersburg to be raised by a wealthy uncle, Henri Terk, and his wife, whose surname she adopted. In 1905, she travelled to Paris, where she enrolled at the progressive Académie de la Palette. A return to Russia was now out of the question for her. After a short-lived marriage of convenience to the art dealer Wilhelm Uhde, she married the artist Robert Delaunay, a man her own age, in 1910. As artists, the two of them inspired each other: the hot-tempered Robert with his greater interest in theory, and the optimistic Sonia with her spontaneous method of working. While he was busy producing his famous series of paintings of a fragmented Eiffel Tower, Sonia concerned herself with creating a home: her first abstract piece of art was a highly colourful coverlet that used scraps of material and was made for her son Charles. A short while later, she adopted equally powerful colour contrasts in her paintings, too, creating spontaneous, free, rhythmical work that verged on abstraction.

'Simultaneity' was the name the Delaunays gave to the new kind of art they developed, painting characterized by the effects of simultaneous contrasts of colour.

On walks along the Boulevard Saint-Michel at night, they observed the effects of new electric streetlights and were prompted by them to experiment with colour. It was during this phase that Delaunay-Terk created one of her most famous works, the 1914 painting *Electric Prisms*, the entire canvas of which is filled with arcs and circular forms in vivid colours spreading outwards from bright centres. The artist juxtaposes pure, strong colours, such as red, blue, green and yellow, and thus achieves a lively interaction of three-dimensional and two-dimensional effects. Henceforth, discs and arcs practically became a trademark of her and her husband's art. She never made it a point of principle to abandon figurative art altogether, however, and often combined it with abstraction.

Like many other married women artists, Delaunay-Terk frequently subordinated her own work to that of her husband whom she regarded as the more important artist. As it was impossible to make a living from avant-garde painting alone, she also began to produce book bindings, cushion covers, clothing and fabric. Her luxurious and uncompromisingly modern designs found enthusiastic buyers in the 1920s, and her fashion-house in Paris developed into a flourishing business with as many as thirty employees and branches in London and Rio de Janeiro. Demand for her work as a designer dwindled during the Great Depression, in the early 1930s, although her work as an artist then began to come into its own.

After her husband's death in 1941, Delaunay-Terk made it her main task to promote his reputation through exhibitions and publications. She herself resumed painting in the 1950s and produced numerous abstract compositions, often tempera on paper, using distinct planes of colour and geometric forms. Sonia Delaunay-Terk produced her last painting, a lively gouache of brilliant red, blue and green, in 1979 at the age of ninety-four.

Sonia Delaunay-Terk
b. 14 November 1885
Gradizhsk, Ukraine
d. 5 December 1979 Paris

- *trained at art colleges in Karlsruhe and Paris*
- *influenced by Paul Gauguin, Vincent van Gogh and the Fauves*
- *friend of the poets Blaise Cendrars and Guillaume Apollinaire*
- *she and her husband designed two pavilions for the 1937 Paris World Fair*
- *made an Officer of the French Legion of Honour in 1975*

Sonia Delaunay-Terk
Electric Prisms, 1914
Oil on canvas, 250 x 250 cm
Musée National d'Art Moderne, Paris

Hannah Höch

A *Cut with the Kitchen Knife Dada through the last Weimar Beer-Belly Cultural Epoch of Germany* is the title of this large-format collage by Hannah Höch. It is a key work of Berlin Dada and an important early example of photomontage. Its very title is programmatic and, in its provocative and playful wording, is typical of Dada usage. The various components of the collage were cut from newspapers, magazines and photographs.

Besides fragments of words and headlines, machine parts, vehicles and urban views, more than fifty figures can be seen in this complex work, although their heads and bodies seldom match. Among them are such famous personalities as the physicist Albert Einstein, Kaiser Wilhelm II, theatre director Max Reinhardt, actress Asta Nielsen and Lenin as well as a number of representatives of Dada, including Höch's companion Raoul Hausmann, the painter George Grosz, the brothers John Heartfield and Wieland Herzfelde. At the centre of this chaotic-looking composition, a female dancer gleefully juggles Käthe Kollwitz's head. The other elements of the collage have been combined with the same sense of freedom and playfulness. Höch has produced a satirical image of the Weimar Republic and its time-honoured and (in the eyes of the Dadaists) meaningless traditions that the group pilloried in their work.

This collage was first seen in 1920 at the 'First International Dada Exhibition' in Berlin – alongside waspish posters, works by Grosz, Hausmann, Max Ernst, Francis Picabia as well as a uniformed dummy with a pig's head and other items that were certain to incense the exhibition's bourgeois visitors. As expected, they did: the press reacted violently and the authorities started proceedings against the organizers for ridiculing the army. Comprising 176 works, this exhibition represented both the climax and the quintessence of the Dada movement that had formed in 1916 in Zurich, Paris,

New York and Berlin as a reaction to the First World War. Together with Hausmann, whom she met in 1915 while studying applied art in Berlin, Höch was one of the original Dadaists. As she later admitted, however, she sometimes felt like the odd 'man' out in this male-dominated group and practically never appeared on stage at their riotous performances. Showing greater subtlety than the others, she exploited the possibilities of collage, made her famous Dada dolls and applied the new technique of montage to her painting.

The Club Dada began to fragment in the early 1920s. Its leading lights – supreme individualists one and all – fell out with each other and went their separate ways. After numerous trial separations and attempts at reconciliation, Höch and Hausmann finally realized in 1922 that their relationship was over. From 1926 to 1929, Höch lived in the Netherlands, where she found a new companion in the avant-garde woman poet Til Brugmann and where she associated with the artists of the De Stijl group. On returning to Germany, she lived through the Nazi era by withdrawing to the leafy Berlin suburb of Heiligensee (where she painted, made collages and tended her overgrown garden). It was not until the end of the 1960s that the work of the aged artist was rediscovered. Although her output was vast and varied, in the eyes of the public Hannah Höch always remained the Dadaist she had been as a young woman.

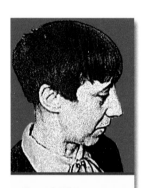

Hannah Höch
b. 1 November 1889
Gotha
d. 31 May 1978 Berlin

- *studied glass making at Berlin's School of Applied Arts and later graphic design under Emil Orlik*
- *maintained ties with Kurt Schwitters, Piet Mondrian and Dutch De Stijl artists*
- *lived with the pianist and economist Kurt Matthies from 1938 to1942*
- *retrospective held in 1971 in Berlin's Academy of Art*

Hannah Höch
A Cut with the Kitchen Knife Dada through the Last Weimar Beer-Belly Cultural Epoch of Germany, 1919-20
Photomontage, 114 x 90 cm
Neue Nationalgalerie, Berlin

Käthe Kollwitz

The life of Käthe Kollwitz spanned more than seventy-five years of political upheaval and social unrest, war and revolution: four years after she was born, the German Empire was proclaimed and just over two weeks after her death, the Second World War came to an end in Europe. Born in Königsberg, East Prussia (now Kaliningrad, Russia), Kollwitz decided early on that graphic art was her preferred medium. It suited her extraordinary talent for drawing and meant that her work was available to a wide range of buyers at an affordable price. Self-referential art was never her thing: 'I should like to exert influences in these times when human beings are so perplexed and in need of help', she wrote in 1922.

In the Berlin working-class district of Prenzlauer Berg, where she lived with her doctor husband Karl Kollwitz, she experienced at first hand the poverty and misery endured daily by the people who lived there. At the start of her career, she executed two series of etchings on historical subjects, the Silesian Weavers' Revolt and the sixteenth-century Peasants' War, in which her gripping, realistic scenes portrayed the suffering and resistance of ordinary folk. These etchings quickly brought her recognition. Kollwitz later concentrated on topical social and political issues, such as unemployment, hunger, child mortality, violence and war. She had already come into contact with socialist thought both through her father, a mason and preacher, and her brother. In 1919, she designed a commemorative print for Karl Liebknecht, the murdered Social Democrat, and participated in exhibitions of workers' art. She herself never belonged to a political party, however.

The lithograph Seed Corn Ought not to Be Ground – the title of which is a quotation taken from Johann Wolfgang von Goethe's 1795–96 novel Wilhelm Meister's Apprenticeship – was her last work of graphic art. It was executed at the beginning of 1942 when, under the Nazi regime, Kollwitz was no longer permitted to show her work in public. With her strong arms and hands, a mother determinedly envelops her children, whose big eyes peek out from beneath her coat. In its symmetrical structure, the motif is reminiscent of medieval images of the Virgin of the Protecting Cloak, but this mother is shielding her children not only from attacks from outside but also from their own thirst for action. These are 'lads, real Berlin lads who, like young horses, get a scent of something and want out there', according to the artist. Her eighteen-year-old son Peter, a volunteer in the First World War, had been killed in Flanders in 1914; her eldest grandson was killed in the Second World War, a few months after the lithograph was completed.

Time and again, Kollwitz turned to the theme of the mother as protectress, mourner and fighter, not only in her woodcuts and lithographs but also in her sculpture. In 1993, an enlarged version of her sculpture Pietà, of 1938, was erected in Karl Friedrich Schinkel's 'Neue Wache' in Berlin to remind future generations of the evils of war and tyranny.

With its clear and powerful imagery and universally understood themes of social protest, the work of Käthe Kollwitz has always met with a wide response. Stylistically, it developed independently of the changing currents of modernism and always remained firmly rooted in its subject. The forceful message of her work occasionally makes the viewer forget just how expertly she employed her artistic means when giving that message form in as convincing a manner as possible.

Käthe Kollwitz
b. 8 July 1867 Königsberg
d. 22 April 1945 Moritzburg near Dresden

- *trained at the Berlin Women Artists' Association*
- *attended sculpture classes in 1904 at the Académie Julian in Paris*
- *made a professor at the Prussian Academy of Arts in Berlin in 1919*
- *pre-eminent 20th-century German woman graphic artist*

opposite
Käthe Kollwitz
Pietà, 1938
Bronze, 36.8 cm high
Käthe-Kollwitz-Museum, Cologne

Käthe Kollwitz
Seed Corn Ought not to Be Ground, 1941-42
Lithograph, 37 x 39.5 cm
Käthe-Kollwitz-Museum, Berlin

Tamara de Lempicka

Her paintings grace glossy calendars, postcards and book jackets, and her portraits of women are as much icons of the 1920s as Bauhaus lamps and tubular steel furniture. Yet Tamara de Lempicka had all but been forgotten when a major retrospective in Paris led to the rediscovery of her work in 1972.

Tamara de Lempicka was an enigmatic figure: while legends about her abound, little serious research has been conducted on her life. In portrait photographs she looks like a glamorous movie star, her eyes raised in the sensual, melancholy fashion of Greta Garbo or Marlene Dietrich. She certainly knew how to put on a show: always flamboyantly dressed, she received her fashionable Parisian clients in a studio boasting modernistic chrome and aluminium furniture and an American bar, everything arranged down to the last detail. She frequented the city's sleazy/chic nightclubs and was known for her numerous affairs with men and women.

Born into the Polish upper classes, in 1916 she married Tadeusz Lempicki, a Russian lawyer. Two years later, they fled the Russian Revolution to Paris, where, without further ado, she appears to have 'ennobled' herself by adding the French 'de' to her name. Initially, she attended the private Académie de la Grande Chaumière, but a greater influence on her was the tuition she received from the Symbolist Maurice Denis and André Lhote, the latter combining the Cubism of Picasso and Braque with an elegant neoclassicism.

Lempicka developed an unmistakable signature that was a perfect complement to the Art Deco style of the inter-war years. She found inspiration not only in the work of Jean-Auguste-Dominique Ingres or Rosalba Carriera, but also in cinema, photography and commercial art. Some of her most famous images, including a self-portrait of her at the wheel of a Bugatti, were originally covers for a women's magazine, *Die Dame*.

The full-length, life-size portrait of the Duchesse de la Salle is one of Lempicka's most important works; in terms of composition and genre, it is influenced by portraits of sixteenth- and seventeenth-century rulers. Her black riding outfit, her self-assured and commanding air, and her smooth, black, short hair lend the duchess markedly androgynous features – only her delicate, manicured hand and red lips accentuate her femininity. There is a sense of restrained sensuality and aggression behind her controlled posture.

Her figure dominates the narrow, angular houses of the townscape behind her, a back-drop often used by the artist. The woman herself has been painted with greater realism than her Cubist-like surroundings, yet she is stylized in typical Lempicka fashion: she has a supple figure that is sharply outlined and her appearance is smooth and hard, almost metal-lic. All in all, the Duchess de la Salle embodies the 'New Woman' who was being promoted in 1920s literature, advertising and fashion pictures.

Lempicka's career peaked at the end of the 1930s. Now Baroness Huffner, she moved to the United States with her second husband in 1939, but in her mature work was never again able to replicate her pre-war successes. She spent the last years of her life in Mexico, where she died in 1980 aged eighty-one.

Tamara de Lempicka
b. 16 May 1898 Warsaw
d. 18 March 1980
Cuernavaca, Mexico

- *first solo exhibition, held in Milan in 1925*
- *in the 1920s contributed regularly to exhibitions such as the Salon des Indépendants*
- *corresponded with the Italian poet Gabriele d'Annunzio*
- *won first prize at the 1927 Exposition Internationale des Beaux-Arts in Bordeaux*

Tamara de Lempicka
The Duchess de la Salle, 1925
Oil on canvas, 161 x 96 cm
Private collection

Georgia O'Keeffe

Georgia O'Keeffe had a way of painting flowers like no other artist before her: close up, magnified, manifold. Seen at this close range, flowers acquire an almost unsettling presence. With its dense brushwork, the smooth surface of *An Orchid* does not try to disguise the material from which it was made, and its curved forms look unfamiliar and abstract. At the same time, they are reminiscent of female anatomy and have erotic associations. Critics and the public have always dwelt on this aspect of O'Keeffe's work, although the artist herself rejected such views. Because flowers are so small, she once said, she chose to paint them big so that people – even busy New Yorkers – would take the time to study them.

Georgia O'Keeffe was raised in a large family on a Wisconsin farm. With the support of her art teacher, she enrolled at the respected Art Institute of Chicago when she was seventeen. Like many women with artistic talent then, she planned to become an art teacher. In 1907 she began studying at the acclaimed, yet conservative, Art Students League in New York at a time when the American art scene very much took its bearings from Europe.

O'Keeffe first encountered modernist art in the form of Paul Cézanne, Henri Matisse and Pablo Picasso in New York's 291 Gallery that was run by the photographer Alfred Stieglitz.

In 1915, she decided to start afresh as an artist and destroyed her early work. Inspired by Wassily Kandinsky's 1911 book entitled *Über das Geistige in der Kunst* (Concerning the Spiritual in Art), she produced some abstract-organic works in charcoal. They delighted Stieglitz who, without the artist's knowledge, exhibited them in his gallery. Going on to become an important promoter of the now thirty-year-old artist, he showed her work almost every year and encouraged her to give up her teaching job. Their professional relationship soon developed into a love affair and they married in 1924. Stieglitz was twenty-three years older than O'Keeffe and

he photographed her almost obsessively, capturing every detail of her body in hundreds of images, and thus helped shape her reputation as a liberal and unconventional woman. O'Keeffe's artwork did not remain untouched by the influence of photography: her canvas-filling flowers are reminiscent of photographic enlargements such as those made by her friend, the photographer Paul Strand.

Following her husband's death in 1946, Georgia O'Keeffe retreated to the New Mexico desert, where she had often spent much of the year since the 1930s. Nature had always been the source of her inspiration as an artist. On her ranch amidst the barren and rocky plateau around Abiquiu, she devoted herself completely to her painting. She would spend hours roaming through the desert studying the expanse of the horizon and collecting sun-bleached bones that she painted with the same cool yet sensuous precision as she did calla lilies, petunias and poppies. When she died shortly before her ninety-ninth birthday, Georgia O'Keeffe, America's most celebrated and successful woman artist, had long been a legend.

Georgia O'Keeffe
b. 15 November 1887 near Sun Prairie, Wisconsin
d. 6 March 1986 Santa Fe, New Mexico

- *foremost American avant-garde artist in addition to Edward Hopper and Marsden Hartley*
- *in 1977, she was awarded the Medal of Freedom, the US's highest decoration*
- *received several honorary doctorates and teaching posts*
- *elected to the American Academy of Arts and Letters, and to the American Academy of Arts and Sciences*

Georgia O'Keeffe
An Orchid, 1941
Pastel, paper on board, 70.2 x 55.2 cm
The Museum of Modern Art, New York

Frida Kahlo

Visitors come and go through Frida Kahlo's bedroom and studio in the 'Blue House' where the Mexican artist was born in 1907 and where she also died. They come to see the four-poster bed on which her painted plaster corset lies, her wheelchair in front of her easel, her diaries and traditional Mexican costumes, the hand-thrown clay bowls in the kitchen and the court-yard adorned with plants. The 'Casa Azul', in the Mexico City suburb of Coyoacán, has been a museum devoted to Kahlo's work since her death in 1954.

There are few artists whom we think we know as well as Frida Kahlo. Her life has been the subject of several films in which we learn what she most liked to eat, what she drank, what the painful details of her history of illness were and how she sympathized with the Communists, how she had various love affairs and what highs and lows she experienced in her marriage to the famous Mexican muralist Diego Rivera, a man twice her age.

The daughter of a successful German-Jewish photographer and a Mexican mother, Frida had originally planned to study medicine. When she was eighteen, however, she was severely injured in a bus accident and was confined to bed for months. This is when she began to paint. Kahlo never received any professional training, however, and from the start, she used painting as a means of examining the accident, its effects on her body and her appearance. Over half her 130-odd paintings are self-portraits. She showed herself wearing different clothes, surrounded by her posses-sions, tropical vegetation or symbolically laden animals, or perforated with nails or in men's clothes, her hair cut short – but always with the same proud bearing and impassive expression of almost mask-like beauty.

Her painting The Two Fridas was executed in 1939 shortly after her divorce from Rivera (yet, this didn't last long, for the two remarried in 1940). A life-size double self-portrait, the paint-ing is unparalleled in the history of art. The 'European' Frida is seen sitting on the left wearing a high-necked, white lacy dress. An artery has been severed and blood drips through the surgical clamp onto her skirt to merge with its embroidered flowers. Her alter ego is the Frida of the darker skin, the one wearing the traditional dress of the Tehuana, just as Rivera loved her. His childhood portrait comes in direct contact with her own lifeblood. This painting is executed simply and realistic-ally – except for the hearts and veins that appear to have been lifted from an anatomical textbook. With such an unexpected conjunction of external reality and internal imagination, Kahlo's painting recalls Surrealist works. When André Breton, the chief spokesman of Surrealism in Paris, 'discovered' her in the late 1930s and introduced her there, she soon distanced herself from the movement. Her work was nourished by sources other than the intel-lectual art of the Surrealists, which, among other things, took its inspiration from psycho-analysis. Above all, Kahlo found her models in the Mexican popular art that she admired and collected, not least its naive votive pictures that juxtapose the unreal and miraculous with the everyday (streams of blood flow from mir-acle-working reliquaries, flaming hearts lie open). Unlike retables, however, Kahlo's pictor-ial world is almost obsessively self-referential. Nowadays she is practically worshipped as a martyr, a proud beauty, a passionate lover and fascinating artist. Especially since the women's movement of the 1980s, she has evolved into a role model.

Frida Kahlo
b. 6 July 1907 Coyoacán, Mexico City
d. 13 July 1954 Coyoacán

- *influenced by Mexican folk art*
- *first solo exhibition, held in New York in 1938*
- *Mexican National Arts and Sciences Award (1946)*
- *married twice to the Mexi-can painter Diego Rivera*
- *most celebrated Mexican and Central American woman artist*

Frida Kahlo
The Two Fridas, 1939
Oil on canvas, 173.5 x 173 cm
Museo de Arte Moderno, Mexico City

Meret Oppenheim

Artists are seldom so much associated with one work as Meret Oppenheim is with her famous *Fur-lined Teacup*. Created in Paris in 1936, this Surrealist object was purchased that same year by the Museum of Modern Art in New York and made its twenty-three-year-old creator famous around the world. None of her later works received anything like the same attention even though, besides sculpture and objects, her varied output included drawings and paintings, furniture designs and poems.

According to the artist, the idea for her fur-covered cup arose quite by chance. In the 1930s, Oppenheim created unusual accessories for the fashion designer Elsa Schiaparelli and one of the pieces she made was a fur-trimmed bangle. The idea of adding a fur trim to other everyday objects came to her during an encounter with Pablo Picasso and his partner Dora Maar at the Café de Flore. When the Surrealists' spokesman, André Breton, asked her a short while later to contribute some thing to an exhibition, Oppenheim translated her idea into action. She bought the cup, saucer and spoon in a Monoprix department store in Paris and covered them in Chinese gazelle hair.

With its unusual combination of materials, the object triggers conflicting thoughts and emotions in viewers. While its soft fur invites them to touch it, the thought of putting it to one's lips instinctively arouses unpleasant sensations. Breton christened the object 'Breakfast in Fur' two years later. 'This meant that part of the scandal it caused was not my own invention', the artist commented later. The name is a reference to the fork lunches had by elegant ladies in furs, but also plays on the work's subliminal eroticism by alluding both to Edouard Manet's famous painting *Le Déjeuner sur l'herbe*, with its naked woman sitting beside two men at a picnic, and Leopold Sacher-Masoch's 1869 erotic novel *Venus in Furs*.

Meret Oppenheim was eighteen when she left Switzerland for Paris, where she wanted to train as an artist. After a short spell at a private art school, she came into contact with the Surrealists around Breton. Man Ray made nude photographs of her and she had an affair with Max Ernst. A young and attractive woman, she quickly became the inspiration for this circle of artists and showed her own work at their exhibitions. Before the imminent outbreak of the Second World War, when the Surrealist group was beginning to disintegrate, Oppenheim returned to Switzerland. Her avant-garde objects met with no response from the culturally more conservative Swiss, however.

The artist remained an outsider and fell into a long depression. It took her until the 1950s to overcome her personal and artistic crisis. She finally broke with the Surrealists in 1959 when Breton asked her to repeat her 'Spring Festival' for the opening of an exhibition. Previously staged in private, this was a banquet upon a woman's naked body. The re-enactment in Paris became a voyeuristic event exclusively for men, however, and Oppenheim felt it completely reversed her original intention of staging a celebration for men and women.

In the early 1970s, the artist put *Fur-lined Teacup* behind her in ironical fashion when she produced a two-dimensional, souvenir-style kitsch version of it that is now also on display in New York's Museum of Modern Art.

Meret Oppenheim
b. 6 October 1913 Berlin
d. 15 November 1985 Basle

- attended the School of Applied Arts, Basle from 1929 to 1930 and in 1937
- first solo exhibition, in Basle in 1936
- retrospective held at Stockholm's Moderna Museet in 1967
- awarded the Art Prize of the City of Basle in 1974 and the Art Prize of the City of Berlin in 1982
- published poetry, dream-inspired drawings and a screenplay

Meret Oppenheim
Fur-lined Teacup (Le Déjeuner en fourrure), 1936
Fur-lined teacup, saucer and spoon, height 7 cm
The Museum of Modern Art, New York

The Twentieth Century

after 1945

Barbara Hepworth

Helen Frankenthaler

Eva Hesse

Niki de Saint Phalle

Hanne Darboven

Louise Bourgeois

Rebecca Horn

Cindy Sherman

Jenny Holzer

Shirin Neshat

Vanessa Beecroft

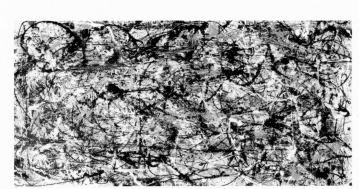

I n the years following the Second World War, the art of Western Europe and the United States was characterized by abstraction. While 'Socialist Realism' was the name given to the officially sanctioned style of art in Eastern bloc countries, in the West, abstract forms were felt to be in keeping with expressions of individualism and freedom. There were many types of abstract art that were variously termed gestural, non-figurative, absolute and concrete. After 1945, artists again picked up the thread of prewar achievements: Kandinsky's abstract painting and his book *Über das Geistige in der Kunst* (Concerning the Spiritual in Art) of 1911, Piet Mondrian's Constructivist style, the investigations into the properties of colour and form at the Bauhaus or the technique of automatism, whereby the Surrealists sought to release creative powers, among them those of the subconscious.

The School of Paris was a seedbed of abstract art in Europe. It included such artists as Alfred Manessier and Pierre Soulages, Hans Hartung and Serge Poliakoff – the latter two German and Russian émigrés in the French capital. After 1945, however, New York superseded Paris as the centre of modern art. Jackson

Pollock's and Willem de Kooning's large, powerful paintings influenced whole generations of artists. Pollock revolutionized art with his Action painting, in which he dribbled paint from cans onto canvases lying on his studio floor, creating thrilling pictures of intertwined and flowing lines. Known as Abstract Expressionism, this type of painting was the result of improvisation and energetic gestural movements. In contrast to Pollock's paintings, de Kooning's expressive and spontaneous work sometimes contains organic and figurative elements. The subsequent generation of Colour Field painters sought greater structure in their work that is distinguished by large expanses of colour. Barnett Newman's large-format abstract paintings have a mystical quality and are composed of monochrome planes of colour. For Mark Rothko, too, colour was the essence of a painting. His expanses of colour have soft, uneven edges and seem to float on the canvas, creating an impression of boundlessness and transcendence. When Ad Reinhardt started to produce his all-black work in the late 1950s, painting seemed to have come to an end.

American Pop art became a force in the 1960s, however. It provided ironic and critical

above left
Mark Rothko
Yellow, Orange, Red on Orange, 1954
Oil on canvas, 292 x 231 cm
Kate Rothko Prizel Collection, New York

above centre
Jackson Pollock
Cathedral, 1947
Enamel and aluminium paint on canvas, 181.6 x 88.9 cm
Dallas Museum of Art, Dallas, Texas

above right
Andy Warhol
Marilyn, 1964
Polymer and screen-printing ink on canvas, 101 x 101.6 cm
Collection of Thomas Amman, Zurich

commentary on contemporary consumerism. Artists such as Andy Warhol and Roy Lichtenstein turned to the banal imagery of advertising and product design, mass media and comic strips, transforming it into poster-like, coloured silkscreen prints, portraits and sculptures. American artist Robert Rauschenberg, a pioneer of Pop art, and the 'Nouveaux Réalistes', among them the Swiss sculptors Jean Tinguely and Daniel Spoerri, created assemblages of everyday objects and junk, thus literally incorporating reality in their work.

Op art, Minimal art and Conceptual art developed during the 1960s as counter-movements to Pop art. The abstract paintings of artists such as Victor Vasarely or Bridget Riley are based on optical effects. In contrast to it, the Minimal art of Sol LeWitt, Carl Andre and Donald Judd was characterized by a limited repertoire of geometrical elements, such as squares or grids. In the 1960s, the international movement of Conceptual art took as its starting point the artist's 'idea', which was felt to be more important than the finished product. The work of the Japanese artist On Kawara, for instance, contains nothing but dates; Joseph Kosuth has people write quotations on walls for him; and Frenchman Daniel Buren uses striped cloth to give rooms and squares an unfamiliar appearance.

In the context of the political demonstrations of the 1960s, whether against the Vietnam War, student protests in Europe or part of the feminist movement, the art scene was also polarized. Joseph Beuys expanded the meaning of art when he declared that 'Everyone is an artist' and proclaimed the unity of art and life. With his performances and room-filling sculptures, but especially with his thoughts on the potential of art to change society, he had a great influence on other artists. In its witty and provocative happenings that expressed its opposition to artistic tradition, the international Fluxus movement revived the spirit of Dada.

After this phase of the internationalization of art, painting – long believed to have been a thing of the past – unexpectedly received new impetus. The 'Neue Wilden' (New Wild Ones) in Germany, Georg Baselitz, for example, conquered the art market with their Neo-Expressionist, large-format works, but in the long term were unable to compete against multimedia art. Internationally, video art gained in importance, and photography also established itself as an independent medium. Installations and serial pieces replaced the single work of art.

Since the 1990s, the art market has been characterized by a plurality of styles and eclecticism. Computer and Internet art is a case in point. In the age of postmodernism, every possible artistic style has been possible, the boundaries of art have been infinitely expanded and crossed, every possible type of provocation has been experienced and all the great examples of art history have been quoted. At the close of the twentieth century, it was barely possible to distinguish general trends among the hotchpotch of artistic positions. Both the art market and art production are linked on a global scale and the role of curators and critics in setting standards and helping to educate the public is becoming ever more important. At the start of the twenty-first century, the latest trend appears to be a revival of painting.

Multimedia Artists

Since a spirit of optimism took hold in the 1960s, women artists have embraced new forms of art such as performance, video and installation that, unlike painting and sculpture, have no art-historical precedents. The feminist movement strengthened women's belief in themselves, increased their awareness of the instruments of power within society and swept away the taboos surrounding the perception of the female body. Artists such as the Austrian Valie Export or the German Ulrike Rosenbach, the star pupil of Joseph Beuys, made experimental films and video installations or staged controversial happenings in public that addressed sexual stereotypes. 'Body art' of the 1970s transformed the body itself into an artistic medium: protagonists such as the Yugoslav artist Marina Abramovic or the Frenchwoman Gina Pane subjected themselves to painful experiences so as to transcend psychological and physical boundaries.

In the 1980s and 1990s, video art evolved from its experimental beginnings into a technically refined, versatile medium as exemplified by the work of the Belgian artist Marie-Jo Lafontaine or the Finnish artist Eija Liisa Ahtila. Photo art also flourished and still does to this day. The Düsseldorf-based artist Katharina Sieverding frequently makes use of

Mona Hatoum, *Homebound*, 2000
Installation, Tate Britain, London

portrait photographs that she distorts and combines in wall-filling works of darkly glowing intensity. A wholly different approach is taken by the photographer Candida Höfer, who submitted work for the German Pavilion at the 2003 Venice Biennale. Taken without the use of artificial light, her large-format, clearly structured, completely objective and neutral photographs are of deserted public buildings such as libraries and museums. The American artist Nan Goldin, on the other hand, became known as the woman who photographed the daily life of drug users, transvestites and prostitutes.

Fields traditionally associated with women, such as textiles, have also been subverted. Rosemarie Trockel, for instance, has made mechanically knitted pictures with recurring patterns of

company logos or political emblems. The Egyptian artist Ghada Amer embroiders on large canvases the outlines of pornographic scenes, which at first sight look like abstractions. Other artists have transformed harmless, everyday objects into installations that prompt distinctly ambiguous sensations in viewers: the French artist Annette Messager, for instance, creates nightmarish scenarios using old cuddly toys, whereas the Palestinian-born artist Mona Hatoum, in her *Homebound* installation, created an ensemble of metal furniture and household objects that were connected by an electrical current, thus transforming the familiar into a source of danger.

At the start of the twenty-first century, (manipulated) computer images are firmly established in the repertoire of young women artists. The star of the art scene is the Swiss Pipilotti Rist. In her colourful, Pop-influenced video *Ever is Over All* from 1997, she uses a huge flower stalk to smash the windscreens of parked cars.

Women have never before played such an important role in art as they do today. In future, too, they will exploit the whole range of media available to them as they open up new perspectives for art.

Events in History: The Twentieth Century after 1945

1948
The state of Israel is proclaimed.

1959
Castro's victory in Cuba intensifies the East-West conflict (missile threat between USA and USSR): peak of the Cold War until 1962.

1961
The Berlin Wall is built, dividing Germany.

1968
Student unrest in Europe and America, initially in reaction to the Vietnam War, reaches its climax. The 'Prague Spring' is suppressed by Warsaw Pact troops.

1969
First moon-landing by the US rocket 'Apollo 11'.

1971
Greenpeace is founded in Vancouver.

1978
The Polish cardinal Karol Wojtyla is elected Pope and takes the name John Paul II.

1989
The Berlin Wall is breached and the Communist system in Europe and the Soviet Union collapses.

1992
The World Wide Web is developed by CERN in Geneva. The number of Internet users rises constantly.

1998-99
Following the collapse of Communism in Eastern Europe, independence movements in the Balkans lead to war in Kosovo.

Barbara Hepworth

Three artists represented Britain at the Venice Biennale in 1950: John Constable, the great 19th-century landscape painter; Matthew Smith, now a little-known 20th-century artist – and the sculptor Dame Barbara Hepworth, then forty-seven years old. Yet this recognition of her work was not without its downside: at the 1948 Biennale, the jury had awarded Henry Moore, a good friend of Hepworth's, the International Sculpture Prize for his block-like, semi-abstract sculptures. Compared with Moore's work, that of the slightly younger Hepworth now seemed to be relegated to a secondary position, much like that of a pupil – which she never was.

They both hailed from Yorkshire and met in 1920 when they were students at Leeds School of Art. Later, too, they were in close contact, especially during the decade before the Second World War, when they both lived in the London suburb of Hampstead, where Hepworth met her second husband, the painter Ben Nicholson. Through exchanges with artist friends like the Constructivists Piet Mondrian and Naum Gabo, Hepworth and Moore came closer to abstraction in their work. Whereas the human body remained an important point of reference for Moore, Hepworth in the 1930s embraced a largely abstract, yet apparently organic, use of forms. Her choice of material – walnut or teak, marble or alabaster, bronze or steel – was an important consideration for her. She loved to carve her forms straight from her block of stone or wood using a hammer or chisel, a technique she had learned together with her first husband, the sculptor John Skeaping, during a study visit to Italy; in England it was not part of a sculptor's training.

The outbreak of the Second World War was a major turning point in Hepworth's life. She left London with her husband, her son Paul and her triplets, to whom she gave birth in 1934, and moved to the Cornish fishing village of St Ives, where she lived for the rest of her life.

Prehistoric standing stones in the dramatic Cornish landscape were her inspiration for new sculptures.

On 11 June 1964, Hepworth's largest sculpture was unveiled in front of the headquarters of the United Nations in New York. Over six metres high, *Single Form* is a memorial to Dag Hammerskjöld, the UN Secretary General who was killed in an aeroplane crash in 1961. Shortly before his death, the Swedish diplomat had discussed with Hepworth, whom he knew personally, the possibility of making a sculpture for the building. Her design made use of a series of similar works from the 1930s. This tall, monolithic, asymmetrical sculpture, with its circular opening, gives rise to different associations: one might think of a human face, a wing, a hand or a shield. Essentially, it is an abstract examination of what Hepworth viewed as the main concern of the winner of the Nobel Peace Prize: his efforts to create order in the face of chaos. In many of her pieces, the tension between mass and space, between organic form and geometric clarity, is central. To this end, she often combined two, three or more elements in one group. Occasionally, she painted the inside of her sculptures to produce a contrast with the natural grain of the wood, or used wires or strings to link the outside and the inside of them, just as Naum Gabo did.

In 1975, Dame Barbara Hepworth died in a fire at her St Ives studio, aged seventy-two. Trewyn Studio is now a museum: her semi-finished blocks of stone still stand in her studio, and finished works, characterized by formal clarity and taut compactness, stand among the trees in her garden. In 2003, the Tate St Ives staged a retrospective to mark the sculptor's centenary.

Barbara Hepworth
b. 10 January 1903
Wakefield, Yorkshire
d. 20 May 1975 St Ives,
Cornwall

- *maintained ties with Brancusi, Braque, Picasso, Mondrian and Arp*
- *in 1933 the only woman in the Abstraction-Création artists' group*
- *work shown at the 'documenta' in Kassel in 1955 and 1959*
- *made a Dame Commander of the Order of the British Empire in 1965*
- *one of the great abstract sculptors of the 20th century*

Barbara Hepworth
Single Form, 1963
Bronze, height 6.40 m
United Nations Plaza, New York

Helen Frankenthaler

Measuring over six-and-a-half by six-and-a-half metres, this painting is overwhelming in size. Its reproduction here suggests it is a water-colour of manageable proportions, but its dimensions have to be grasped before its effect can be appreciated. The artist Helen Frankenthaler prefers large formats; for this painting, she unrolled a huge, unprimed canvas across the floor of her New York studio in 1958. Choosing not to use brushes as conventional painting on canvas required, she instead diluted her oils with turpentine until they were as liquid as water. Using coffee pots, she then poured her thinned-down paint across her canvas in great sweeps. Dark green and strong red seeped into the canvas and left lines of colour behind, while brilliant yellow-ochre formed cloud-like patches. Blue-grey and earthy-brown shades were also added. The canvas fibres soaked up the paint and combined with the pigment to form a unity of support and media. The viewer's gaze takes in the lively movement of the trails of paint, grasping the dynamism of the painting process.

Helen Frankenthaler's works are about the act of painting itself. While they are abstract, free, artistic improvisations, the viewer can also see suggestions of figurative art in them, forms that are both ambiguous and reminiscent of nature or even numerals. The title of the paint-ing, *Before the Caves*, gives a clue as to the source of the artist's inspiration. A few years earlier, she had travelled to northern Spain to see the prehistoric cave paintings at Altamira with their earth-coloured images of animals. They impressed her greatly and her painting is a very free, associative reference to them. The com-bination of figurative art and pure abstraction is typical of Frankenthaler's work.

The daughter of a wealthy New York family, Frankenthaler completed her art studies at Columbia University when she was in her early 1920s and moved into her own studio in Chelsea, a part of town popular among artists.

In the years after the Second World War, New York developed into the world's leading art centre. A whole generation of young artists was spellbound by Jackson Pollock's sensational Action painting, in which he poured and dripped his paint from cans onto canvases laid on the floor. Taking a lively interest in the artis-tic debates and experiments of the early 1950s, Frankenthaler visited Pollock and his wife, Lee Krasner, in their studio, associated with Willem and Elaine de Kooning and was in close contact with the art critic Clement Greenberg, who was an important advocate of Abstract Expressionsm. Frankenthaler quickly developed her own unmistakable style of painting, however, which was indebted to her examina-tion of Wassily Kandinsky's early abstract works. A crucial aspect of it was the technique she developed of allowing her paint to soak into unprimed canvas. For American artists like Kenneth Noland and Morris Louis, this new painting technique amounted to a revolution and they adopted it immediately in their abstract paintings and developed it. One of the most innovative and influential artists of her generation, Helen Frankenthaler still lives in New York.

Helen Frankenthaler
b. 12 December 1928
New York
lives in New York

- *important representative of Abstract Expressionism*
- *married artist Robert Motherwell in 1958 (divorced in 1971)*
- *teaching posts from 1959 in New York, Yale, Princeton and Harvard*
- *in 1966 was one of four artists to represent the United States at the Venice Biennale*
- *in 1990 elected to the American Academy of Arts and Letters*

Helen Frankenthaler
Before the Caves, 1958
Oil on canvas, 260 x 265 cm
University of California, Berkeley Art Museum, Berkeley

Eva Hesse

'My attitude toward art is most open. It is totally unconservative – just freedom and willingness to work. I really walk on the edge... And if I'm not quite there yet, that's where I'm headed for... This is just the start...', Eva Hesse said in an interview in 1970. That same year she died of cancer, aged thirty-four. The myth of Eva Hesse, the young artist who died tragically young, has crucially influenced the perception of her work, as indeed has the rapid publication of her diaries. In 1939, when she was three years old, she and her German-Jewish family had to flee the Nazis. They quit Hamburg for New York, where her parents separated and her mother committed suicide. Although constant fears, doubts and crises shaped her state of mind, Hesse nonetheless created a body of work of great power and individualism. To this day, it is an important source of inspiration for other artists.

She started out as a painter, but because she felt the results were unsatisfactory, she took up drawing. However, her breakthrough as an artist came only when she turned her hand to sculpture – the medium of her mature work. She did so in 1964, when she was in Germany for over a year together with her husband, the sculptor Tom Doyle, who had received an invitation from a textile manufacturer to work in the Rhineland. Earlier than other American artists, she was able to examine contemporary European art: the work of Joseph Beuys, the punctured canvases of Lucio Fontana, Günther Uecker's nail pieces. Back in New York after 1965, she quickly made a name for herself with her objects. She adopted the geometrical permutations of Carl Andre's or Sol LeWitt's minimal art and combined them with oddly shaped structures and unusual materials that were not part of art's conventional repertory: flex, wire, latex, glass-fibre, cast resin or rubber tubing – everyday, 'nasty', unexceptional materials of indeterminate colour and often of soft or elastic texture. Her choice of material opened up new horizons for twentieth-century sculpture. Produced in 1967-68, *Accession* III is one of her best-known works, although Hesse herself later felt it to be too attractive, too linear and perfect. It is a cube of opaque fibreglass measuring 80 · 80 · 80 cm, and its sides are perforated with rows of holes. It is an object with an unambiguous shape, one that is severe and mathematically precise, much like a manufactured part. Confusion arises, however, when the viewer sees the inside of the cube that is open at the top. There can be no talk of geometric order here! Embedded in the cube's perforated walls are thousands of short pieces of tubing that project into its semi-dark interior; being elastic, they bend downwards and create an impression of something organic – such as tiny tentacles. Like many other works by Hesse, this one is decidedly ambiguous in its combination of hard and soft, rigidity and plasticity, geometric and organic forms. The cube is central to her work and represents her basic desire to achieve order and regularity, which, however, she offset with openness, incalculability and free form.

Eva Hesse
b. 11 January 1936
Hamburg
d. 29 May 1970 New York

- *emigrated to the US with her family in 1938*
- *received teaching post in 1968 at School of Visual Arts, New York*
- *first solo exhibition, held in New York in 1963*
- *retrospective held in Guggenheim Museum, New York, in 1972*

Eva Hesse
Accession III, 1967-68
Fibreglas, 80 x 80 x 80 cm
Museum Ludwig, Cologne

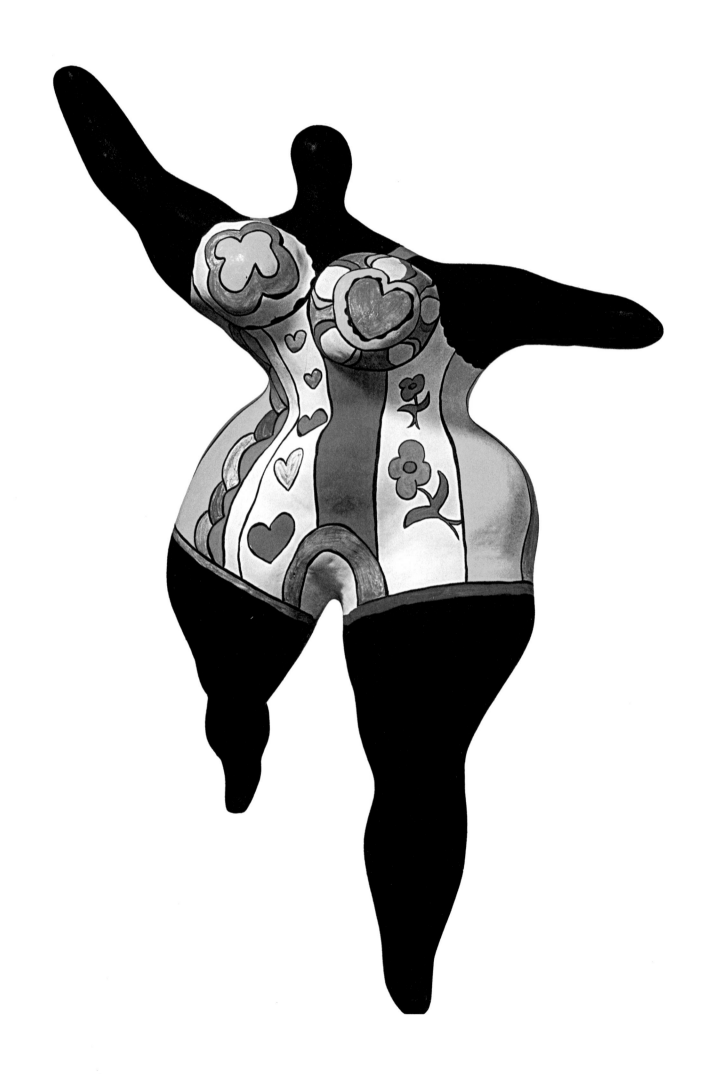

Niki de Saint Phalle

It's 12 February 1961; the place: Paris. Some artists have gathered in a squalid cul-de-sac in Montparnasse, among them Jean Tinguely and Daniel Spoerri, along with the gallery owner Jeannine de Goldschmidt and the critic Pierre Restany. The thirty-one-year-old Niki de Saint Phalle steps forward and takes aim at a white plaster relief leaning against a gable end. Containers of paint embedded in the plaster burst when hit and streams of red, blue and green paint run down the relief.

This was the first of more than a dozen 'rifle-shot' paintings made by Niki de Saint Phalle, and it marked her breakthrough as an artist. Restany invited her to join a group he had founded, the 'Nouveaux réalistes', whose work made use of everyday objects, scrap and other materials. Their intention was to lend art a new sense of reality and to disassociate themselves from the main artistic current of the day, Abstract Expressionism. Niki de Saint Phalle then came into contact with such artists as Arman, Christo, Jasper Johns, Yves Klein and Robert Rauschenberg.

The 'rifle-shot' paintings were an act of release for the artist because they allowed her to vent her pent-up aggression – particularly towards her father and the male-dominated society in which she lived – in a playful, creative way. The daughter of a French aristocrat and an American mother, Niki de Saint Phalle was raised in France and the United States in an environment marked by strict Catholicism and conservative values. On finishing school, she worked as a model for fashion magazines like Harper's Bazar and Vogue. Aged nineteen, she married the budding author Harry Matthews and soon gave birth to two children. She executed her first oils without having had any professional training, but it was only after suffering a nervous breakdown that she finally decided, in 1953, to become an artist. She left her husband and children in 1960 and moved into a studio with the Swiss sculptor and experimental artist Jean Tinguely. They collaborated as artists and eventually married.

In 1963, she embarked on an examination of female role models, such as mother, whore, witch and bride, and created bizarre female sculptures made of wire netting, papier-mâché, plastic dolls, fabric and plaster. Inspired by the pregnant wife of an artist friend of hers, the painter Larry Rivers, Saint Phalle in 1964 created the first of her 'Nanas', full-figured, light-footed female sculptures painted in bold, imaginative colours that became her trademark. As the women's movement developed, they also became icons of women's new self-confidence. The 'Nanas' radiate optimism, a zest for life and powerful sensuality, their forms reminiscent both of Pop art and ancient female fertility symbols. Later in her career, the artist's work increasingly alluded to esoteric teachings, such as the Jewish Cabbala, Mexican mythology and Christian concepts of paradise and hell. She viewed her sculptures as archetypes of the sort described by the psychoanalyst C. G. Jung: embodiments of the collective unconscious.

With her highly distinctive work, Saint Phalle is one of the twentieth century's most popular women artists. Those who engage with her work are transported from the hi-tech present to a latter-day fairy-tale world. In Jerusalem, her *Golem* is a children's playground slide; in Paris, her *Stravinsky Fountain*, a collaboration between her and Tinguely, graces the square in front of the Centre Pompidou. Her tour de force, however, is the *Tarot Garden*, which has been drawing visitors to the remote south-west corner of Tuscany since 1998. Niki de Saint Phalle died in spring 2002, aged seventy-one.

Niki de Saint Phalle
b. 29 October 1930
Neuilly-sur-Seine
d. 22 May 2002 San
Diego

- *exhibitions in Amsterdam, Stockholm, Paris and New York after 1961*
- *designed French Pavilion at 'Expo '67' in Montreal*
- *retrospective held at Musée d'Art Moderne, Paris (Centre Pompidou), 1980*
- *moved to California in 1994*

Niki de Saint Phalle
Dancing Black Nana, 1965-66
Polyester, *height approx.* 200 cm
Private collection

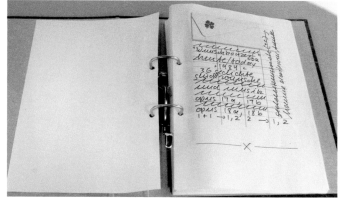

above
Hanne Darboven
Solo for Double Base, 1984
Installation
documenta XI, Kassel, 2002

right
Hanne Darboven
Request Concert, 1984
Installation
documenta XI, Kassel, 2002

Hanne Darboven

Hanne Darboven's studio in Hamburg contains finds of all kinds: ships' models, figures of animals, landscape paintings, portrait busts, framed prints, a flying angel and a skeleton. A rich fund of pictures and objects surrounds the artist there. Her own work, however, is sparse, austere, ascetic almost. Writing is her craft, although she does not compose literary texts, but abstract notations, rows of numbers and mathematical calculations using dates. In her own words: 'I write, but describe nothing'. Each of her works contains hundreds or thousands of closely filled sheets of paper that she assembles in wall-filling installations or publishes in thick tomes.

Since the end of the 1960s, she has produced a body of work that is now barely manageable in size. It has been seen in numerous solo exhibitions in Amsterdam and New York, Paris and Chicago. Since 1972, Darboven has been shown four times at the *documenta*, a major forum for contemporary art, staged in the German city of Kassel. The curator of the 2002 exhibition, New York-based Okwui Enwezor, made her work one of its central features. Taking up three floors, *Solo for Double Base* comprises almost 4,500 sheets of typewritten rows of numbers, arranged according to a rigorous system that is not immediately clear to the viewer. Her *Request Concert* was shown alongside it in display cases; it combines historical greetings cards and numerical sequences in wavelike rows of lines. The titles of both works make reference to music, which plays an important role in Darboven's creative output. She has also translated numerical transcriptions into musical notation with the result that Solo for Double Base, for instance, can be performed as a piece of 'mathematical music', as Darboven puts it. As a piece of written work, the sheer extent of *Solo for Double Base* is overwhelming; it is fascinating both for the clarity of its underlying idea and its disciplined execution. Darboven rejects any kind of spontaneity in her work and does not address the viewer's emotions. Her cool, rational art demands a high degree of concentration from those viewing it and it can also be understood as a protest against the flood of images and information associated with today's mass media.

Hanne Darboven comes from a line of German entrepreneurs who made their money in the cocoa and coffee trade. She was born in 1941 and worked for a while as a pianist; in 1963, however, she enrolled at Hamburg's Academy of Art, where she studied under Almir da Mavignier, a Brazilian practitioner of Op art. In 1966, she moved to New York for two years and there came into contact with exponents of Minimal art, such as Carl Andre and Sol LeWitt. She began filling sheets of graph paper with geometric drawings, but soon eschewed them in favour of numerical sequences – on which she has concentrated since. In what followed, particularly A *Month, a Year, a Century*, she found the main thrust of her work as a creative artist: an investigation of the passage of time. Later on, she began to include political and historical artefacts – postcards, photographs, quotations or everyday objects – in her work, examples being B*ismarck-Time* or *Cultural History*. Moreover certain groups of works are dedicated to personalities, such as Jean-Paul Sartre, Johann Wolfgang von Goethe or Rainer Werner Fassbinder. Together with such artists as the Japanese On Kawara or the Pole Roman Opalka, who are also interested in the visualization of time, Hanne Darboven is now one of the pre-eminent representatives of Conceptual art.

Hanne Darboven
b. 29 April 1941 Munich
lives in Hamburg

- *first solo exhibition, held at Galerie Konrad Fischer, Düsseldorf, in 1967*
- *international reputation since showing at Conceptual art exhibition 'When Attitudes Become Form' in Berne, 1969*
- *her piece '12 Monate, Europaarbeit' has been on permanent display in the Reichstag in Berlin since 1999*
- *awarded the Edwin Scharff Prize of Hamburg in 1986*

Louise Bourgeois

Louise Bourgeois
b. 25 December 1911 Paris
lives in New York

- *studied at the Ecole des Beaux-Arts, under Julius Bissier and Fernand Léger*
- *work contains references to Rodin, Brancusi and Surrealism*
- *at the age of 70, she is given a major retrospective at the Museum of Modern Art in New York*
- *awarded the Golden Lion at the 1999 Venice Biennale*

A room only of doors, a cell too small to walk into: a stage for the imagination. The steel doors with their hinged, solid windows and locks are reminiscent of a prison and give rise to a sense of claustrophobia. Some are closed, others are barely ajar, some are open and afford the viewer a glimpse inside the blue hexagon. In it stands a massive block of marble from whose rough surface a pair of finely worked hands and lower arms rise. They are utterly life-like, their veins and bones seen below the surface. These fragments of a body appear to have a life of their own and are evocative of dreams or surreal pictures. The gesture made by these hands is ambiguous and is not taken from the usual art-historical repertoire. Are the two sets of fingers being dug into each other or are they caressing each other? A round, swivelling mirror resembles a large, vigilant eye and suggests an operation. Louise Bourgeois's confined *Cell* appears to be highly charged with personal reminiscence and a wealth of possible associations. Is this about love and death, about imprisonment and flight or about experiences of physical closeness or physical distance?

The ambiguity of this installation is typical of the artist's work, especially her large group of works titled *Cells* that she started aged seventy-five. Bourgeois herself often explains her work by referring to her childhood that she draws on for inspiration: 'It is the events that happened [in my early childhood] that are the source of my sculptures. My work deals with problems. What the shape of this problem is is what the sculptures are really about.'

Born in Paris in 1911, even as a girl Bourgeois experienced art as something 'useful': her parents dealt in and restored antique tapestries. The ten-year-long affair her father had with the family's governess was a childhood experience that left its mark on Bourgeois, and it became the focus of her mature work.

First, however, she went to university in 1932 to study mathematics as she was fascinated by geometry. She was twenty-five before she switched to art. In 1938, Bourgeois moved to New York with her husband, the American art historian Robert Goldwater, and she lives and works there to this day. It was in 1940s New York that she first exhibited her early, stela-like sculptures. She later began to work in marble and, along with Eva Hesse, was one of the first artists in the 1960s to use formless materials such as latex and rubber. Her sculptures are often erotic and androgynous in appearance. She has also produced an extensive body of graphic work. Her *Insomnia Drawings*, the result of sleepless nights, were shown at the 2002 documenta in Kassel.

Although the artist mainly uses her work to address personal issues, its significance is not lost in its autobiographical elements. From her experiences and emotions Bourgeois extracts poetic visual metaphors that appeal directly to those viewing them. As the ninety-one-year-old artist commented in an interview with Katrin Wittneven on the occasion of her 2003 retrospective in Berlin: 'You don't need to know anything about my biography when you look at the work. It either communicates to you or not. My work deals with emotions that are universal.'

Louise Bourgeois
Cell (Hands and Mirror), 1995
Installation, 160 x 122 x 114 cm
Cheim & Read Gallery, New York

Rebecca Horn

Her installations have been seen in the forbidding ruins of a prison tower in Münster, the Chapelle Saint-Louis de la Salpêtrière in Paris, a Renaissance villa in Tuscany, the theatre of a Viennese asylum and an old primary school in Kassel. Born in 1944 in the southern German town of Michelstadt, Rebecca Horn alludes in her works to the mood of the space in which they are shown – be it a historic building, the neutral rooms of a gallery or a museum such as the National Gallery in London. When a retrospective of her work was held in New York's Guggenhein Museum, she said she wanted her sculptures to make the secret music of particular spaces audible.

For her 1992 installation *El rio de la luna* (*River of the Moon*) in a former hat factory in Barcelona, the artist had mercury flow through long, winding lead pipes and pumped into metal chambers representing the ventricles of a heart. They contained the keys to seven rooms in an old hotel with rooms to let by the hour and where the other part of the installation was on show. Horn had modified the rooms only sparingly and transformed them into the seven stations of an 'essay' on love. Partly in poetic and partly in dramatic terms, she made tenderness, romance and light-heartedness, but also aggression and isolation, the subject of her installation. In the 'Room of Lovers', for instance, tiny motors drove violins that had alighted on the walls and furniture like mechanical butterflies; in the 'Room of Air', wings made of red feathers moved up and down; in the 'Room of the Circle', a metal nail several metres in length scraped the walls; in the 'Room of Water', a bed suspended from the ceiling dripped liquid into glass funnels; and in the 'Room of Mutual Destruction', two movable pistols that were aimed at each other were installed in untidy beds in readiness for a fatal duel, in readiness for the 'Kiss of Death'.

As a student, Horn had lived for a time in Barcelona's cheap Hotel Peninsula. The installation she produced decades later is typical of her work, which often makes use of personal experience, but also takes its inspiration from the work of Marcel Duchamp and Joseph Beuys, the literature of Jean-Paul Sartre and Franz Kafka or the films of Pier Paolo Pasolini and Federico Fellini.

In 1972, she was one of the youngest artists to participate in *documenta* V in Kassel; even her early performances that she showed there were inspired by personal experiences. As a twenty-one-year-old student at Hamburg School of Art, she severely damaged her lungs when working with polyester and fibreglass and she had to spend a long time recuperating in a sanatorium. Following this period of isolation, she began to investigate physical and spatial experiences in performances for which she made special objects such as extra-long gloves, feather masks or fans attached to and operated by her body. She made films and videos of her performances and, in 1978, also started to make feature films, such as *Der Eintänzer* (1978), *La Ferdinanda* (1981) or *Buster's Bedroom* (1990), in which she first used mechanical sculptures like the *Peacock Machine* or the tango-dancing table. Using electric motors, the artist gives inanimate objects a life of their own and has them perform actions that convey to the viewer the tension that exists between vulnerability and aggression. They are perpetual rituals of love, desire, hate and isolation.

Rebecca Horn
b. 1944 Michelstadt, Odenwald, Germany

- *attends St Martin's School of Art in London in 1971*
- *prize-winner at the 1986 'documenta' in Kassel, Karlsruhe Multimedia art prize, 1992*
- *professor at Berlin's School of Art (Universität der Künste) since 1989*
- *writes poetry in addition to screenplays*

Rebecca Horn
El rio de la luna: Room of Lovers, 1992
Installation
Hotel Peninsula, Barcelona

Cindy Sherman

Cindy Sherman creates masterly *mises en scène* in her photographs. Her still lifes, for instance, can be so nauseating that the sight of them can cause viewers to feel sick. Yet her images of sweets and mouldy leftovers possess colours so beautiful that they almost befit Old Masters paintings. She has produced grotesque and macabre photographs using prosthetic body parts and dolls and, in 1997, made *Office Killer*, her first movie.

Cindy Sherman achieved fame with a series of photographs in which she was her own subject. Since the 1970s, she has posed in front of the camera countless times, but not one of her photographs is a self-portrait in the conventional sense. She uses different backdrops and props, dons costumes and masks, trowels on layers of make-up, slips on wigs, false noses and breasts. The real Sherman

always remains hidden. She once commented that her images were personified feelings with their very own natures, ones that represented themselves and not her.

Even as a little girl, Sherman loved to dress up at home, in Glen Ridge, New Jersey, where she was born in 1954. Because of her obvious gift for drawing, she studied art at State University College in Buffalo and, together with fellow students Robert Longo and Nancy Dwyer, opened the Hallwalls Gallery. She

moved to New York in 1978 and soon met her husband-to-be there, the French video artist Michel Auder.

Produced between 1977 and 1980, her *Untitled Film Stills* is an extensive series of black-and-white photographs, each measuring roughly 20 x 25 cm. Sherman is the sole protagonist in every photograph, whether she is seen in the kitchen, at night by the roadside or in a rumpled bed. At times we see her in a neat suit and a blonde wig, at others wearing an apron or in a petticoat. Thematic and formal associations between the individual photographs are suggested, but remain vague: these are stills from movies that were never made. In *Film Still # 4*, a woman, her eyes closed, is shown leaning against a door in a bare and dimly lit corridor, the image reminiscent of 1950s and 1960s movies. In its emotional content, the scene appears neutral and ambiguous; every attempt to develop a storyline fails for lack of any discernible anecdotal or narrative clues. The only thing that is apparent is the picture's artificial nature. Sherman's *Film Stills* demonstrate the absurdity of the long-held belief that photographs reproduce reality; rather than reality, they reflect common clichés and stereotypes.

In the 1980s, Sherman concentrated on fashion and fashion photography, whose standards of beauty she exposed to ridicule in her constructed scenarios. This was the era of her famous *History Portraits*, in which she recreated famous paintings from the Renaissance to Picasso as photographs. In her masquerades, Sherman also questions our ideas concerning the artist's authentic self, and the individual, unmistakable personality as a social construct.

Her concern with idealized images of femininity and beauty has earned Sherman the reputation of being a feminist artist, a label from which she has increasingly distanced herself with her 1990s scenarios on themes of horror and detritus.

Cindy Sherman
b. 1954 Glen Ridge,
New Jersey
lives in New York

■ *solo exhibition at Whitney Museum of American Art, New York, 1987*
■ *shows at the 1982 and 1995 Venice Biennale and at the 1982 'documenta' in Kassel*
■ *her staged photographs make her one of the most outstanding photographic artists of our time*

opposite
Cindy Sherman
Untitled Film Still # 21, 1978
Gelatin silver print, 20 x 25 cm

The Museum of Modern Art, New York
above
Cindy Sherman
Untitled Film Still # 4, 1977
Gelatin silver print, 20 x 25 cm
The Museum of Modern Art, New York

Jenny Holzer

The work of American artist Jenny Holzer makes use of a variety of popular media: posters, peaked caps, packets of condoms, television, LED displays and, since 1995, the Internet. Best known of all are her computer-controlled LED displays that she started making in 1982.

Jenny Holzer was born in Ohio in 1950, the daughter of a car dealer and a riding instructor. She began her career as an abstract artist influenced by the Color Field paintings of Morris Louis and Mark Rothko before finding an original form of expression in 1977 when she placed the written word at the heart of her work. Her first series, *Truisms*, comprised one-liners such as 'Abuse of power comes as no surprise' or 'Freedom is a luxury not a necessity' that she printed on T-shirts and posters. There are more than 250 one-liners in the series. They do not reflect her personal beliefs, but instead are intended, in a kind of parody, to reproduce the 'great ideas of Western thought' in abbreviated form – contradictions and all. Placed in public spaces, her one-liners were designed to make people stop and think.

Her *Truisms* form the basis of a rich fund of texts that are quite disparate in nature; expanded continually ever since, her *Truisms* are now displayed in large-scale installations in museums, sometimes simultaneously. Holzer's *Inflammatory Essays*, produced from 1979 to 1982, consist of one hundred words each and are inspired by political and religious thought. She lent her *Laments* of 1989 a more personal note, making them less trite and more thoughtful and poetic. Holzer's work frequently addresses the issues of physical and psychological abuse, as exemplified by the shockingly realistic texts of her 1992 *War* series, produced in reaction to the first Gulf War, and in *Lustmord* of 1996, a work she was compelled to make on hearing about the many rapes and sexually motivated murders (*Lustmord*) of women in Bosnia. Holzer's work is also inspired by

personal experiences, however: following the birth of her daughter Lili, she produced her *Mother and Child* series in 1990. Her OH series from 2001 also relates to a mother's feelings, physical sensations, tenderness and fear.

With her fly-posting activities at the start of her career, Holzer operated outside the bounds of traditional art, but since the late 1980s, she has also submitted ever grander installations to major galleries, where the subversive power of her work is less apparent than her ability to stage her art in impressive settings. For her 1989–90 retrospective in New York's Guggenheim Museum, she had an LED sign attached to Frank Lloyd Wright's spiral walkway, and thus achieved a highly suggestive and dramatic effect with her 330 messages that took almost two hours to run through.

Holzer's work has always commanded widespread interest, be it her huge LED display in New York's Times Square in 1982 or her installation in Germany's New National Gallery in Berlin, which she illuminated with her electronic messages. In the course of her career, Holzer has made increasingly skilful use of the aesthetic possibilities of LED displays and lasers, making of her messages a kind of visual music for those who read them.

Jenny Holzer
b. 29 July 1950 -
Gallipolis, Ohio
lives in New York

- *studied art in Ohio, Chicago and New York, from 1968 to 1977*
- *has used granite benches and plaques for her messages since 1985*
- *exhibited at the 1987 'documenta' in Kassel*
- *her design for the American Pavilion at the 1990 Venice Biennale won her the Golden Lion*

Jenny Holzer
Untitled, 1989
Installation
Solomon R. Guggenheim Museum, New York

Shirin Neshat
Untitled (from the series *Rapture – Women Scattered*), 1999
Gelatin silver print, 108 x 171 cm
The Cleveland Museum of Art, Metropolitan Bank Collection, Cleveland, Ohio

Shirin Neshat

Shirin Neshat was born in 1957 in Kasvin, north central Iran. Her father, a doctor, approved of Reza Shah Pahlavi's efforts to modernize his country and open it to Western influences. Neshat's parents were wealthy and were able to give their five children an education abroad. Shirin Neshat began to study painting at the University of California at Berkeley in 1974. She was prevented from returning home by Iran's fundamentalist revolution of 1979, in which the country became an Islamic republic under the leadership of Ayatollah Khomeini.

Neshat moved to New York and at first ran the not-for-profit 'Storefront for Art and Architecture', a gallery that belonged to her husband, the Korean architect and Conceptual artist Kyong Park. She did not return to Iran until 1990, a year after Khomeini's death, and was shocked to see the changes in Iranian society, particularly the ways in which women's lives had become strictly regimented. They were forbidden from leaving their homes unless veiled, for instance. What she saw prompted Neshat, after a break of ten years, to resume work as an artist, but this time she chose photography, rather than painting, as her medium.

Her 1993–97 series of photographs titled *Women of Allah* made her international reputation. These clearly structured black-and-white photographs depict women wearing the traditional, full-length *chadar*. Their exposed hands, face and feet are decorated with script resembling tattoos, but the photographs have in fact been overwritten in ink. Of course, most Western viewers are unaware that these texts are written in Farsi, the official language of Iran. Like enigmatic, decorative calligraphy from another world, they represent the work of Iranian women writers

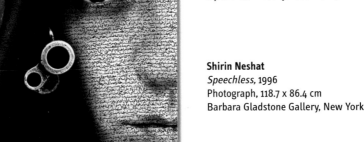

and they deal with sensuality and sexuality. For this reason Neshat has so far been unable to show her work in Iran itself. In some of Neshat's photographs, women – often the artist herself – are shown holding the barrel of a gun or cartridge cases. With her images of proud and militant women, the artist undermines widespread Western notions about oppressed and passive women in Islamic societies.

Since 1997, Neshat's main medium has been video. She often makes use of two projection screens opposite each other, as she does in her thirteen-minute-long video *Rapture*, whose sublime aesthetic entrances viewers. Produced in black-and-white, the pace of its narration is slow, its backdrops and plot seemingly archaic and timeless. In contrast to American or European cinema, individuals are not the focus of the film. Instead, men and women act in impressively choreographed crowd scenes whose insurmountable polarity immediately becomes apparent. Clad in *chadars*, the women move through a barren landscape, while the men, also dressed uniformly, in white shirts and dark trousers, enter a deserted fortress, where they perform ablutions and recite prayers. The underlying message is clear: the domain of culture and religion is a male one; women are excluded from it. While the men adhere to tradition, the women head for the coast, where some of them step into a boat that they row out to sea. Is this suicide or a departure towards new shores? Despite her use of what at first glance appears to be graphic imagery, the artist leaves her other works open to interpretation, too.

Shirin Neshat
Speechless, 1996
Photograph, 118.7 x 86.4 cm
Barbara Gladstone Gallery, New York

Shirin Neshat
b. 1957 Kasvin, Iran
lives in New York

- *she examines the roles of men and women in Islamic society*
- *international shows since 1995, e.g. in Venice, Istanbul, Sydney, Johannesburg, New York*
- *awarded the Golden Lion at the 1999 Venice Biennale*
- *exhibited her work at the 2002 'documenta', Kassel*

Vanessa Beecroft

Vanessa Beecroft
b. 1969 Genoa
lives in New York

- *graduated from the Accademia di Brera in Milan in 1994*
- *has held performances in various cities since 1994, including New York, Bordeaux, Philadelphia, Boston, Stockholm, Leipzig and Sydney*
- *shows at the 1997 and 2001 Venice Biennale*

Born in Genoa, Italy, in 1969, Vanessa Beecroft experienced a meteoric rise to fame in the art world. She was twenty-four when she had her first exhibition and, only five years later, her work was on display in New York's renowned Guggenheim Museum. Photographs of her performances fetch large sums of money at art fairs and auctions; on 30 June 2000, Sotheby's in London sold one of her photographs for more than £30,000!

Beecroft's 'medium' is usually young women, who appear in her performances either scantily clad or naked. 'I regard them as subjects of a painting,' says the artist. 'There is a design of the performance before it happens, made by colours and numbers... The girls always change it during the four to five hours' time they are installed. I get disappointed, but it is the gap between what I'm expecting and what happens that I'm interested in.'

The daughter of an Englishman and an Italian professor of literature, Beecroft spent the first four years of her life in London. When her parents separated, she went to live with her mother near Lake Garda in northern Italy. She later studied classical art, architecture and stage design in Genoa and Milan. For her first exhibition in Milan's Galerie Inga Pinn, in 1993, Beecroft showed watercolour drawings and excerpts from a diary that described her struggle with an eating disorder – while thirty specially chosen young women mingled with the guests. This staged installation established the boundaries of her work. In subsequent performances, she refined and varied her technique. She hired long-legged models of perfect proportions and installed them wearing designer lingerie and high heels. Wearing wigs and make-up, her models all looked similar and anonymous, underlining the artificiality of their performance. The artist instructed them to avoid eye contact with the spectators, not to speak and to remain motionless whenever possible.

Beecroft's discovery by influential New York gallery owners, such as Jeffrey Deitch and, later, Larry Gagosian, paved the way for her admission to the great museums of contemporary art.

At her VB 35 performance in the Guggenheim Museum in 1998, fifteen tall, slender models appeared in glittering Gucci bikinis alongside five other women who were naked except for their stilettos. The effect was striking: the 'show', as Beecroft called it, was reminiscent of fashion shows or contemporary theatre performances, but at the same time the women seemed like mannequins or classical sculptures, their high heels the pedestals of today. During the performance, the originally planned strict order of events disintegrated, and some of the women crouched or sat down on the ground. The models' nudity in the museum setting was a source of irritation, but it fell short of the shock effect associated with the happenings of Performance art (Fluxus, for instance) and Body art in the 1970s and 1980s. While it attacks artistic tradition and social norms, Beecroft's work deals with contemporary trends in culture, such as the prevailing ideal of beauty and the cult of body in advertising – without openly criticizing them, however. The artist's work is also inspired by film, literature and current events.

Reactions to Beecroft's provocative installations vary: some critics see her as a radical exponent of Performance art who has redefined the role of the nude in art, while others describe her work as voyeuristic and peddling clichéd images of women as objects of sexual desire.

Vanessa Beecroft
Show, 1998
Photographs of the performance
Solomon R. Guggenheim Museum, New York

Glossary

Abstract Expressionism: A blanket term for various non-figurative trends in painting in the 1940s, 1950s and 1960s, in which expression and meaning are conveyed solely by colour, form and manner of painting.

Abstraction: Non naturalistic, sometimes completely non-representational, imagery.

Action painting: A manner of painting in which, without a preliminary sketch, the paint is brushed, dripped or slung on to the canvas, which may be placed on the floor. Pictorial structures result from intuitive control of the painting process and from the way the paint 'behaves', taking the form of random drips etc.

Art Nouveau: Stylistic movement around 1900 characterized by a linear, ornamental and decorative formal vocabulary. Known as Jugendstil in Germany and Austria, where it is sometimes also called Sezessionsstil.

Assemblage: Work of art incorporating three-dimensional everyday objects or fragments of objects, which are generally unchanged by the artist. The first assemblages were made by Kurt Schwitters in the 1910s.

Automatism: Spontaneous technique of painting and writing, employed without rational, moral or aesthetic control, as by the Surrealists and exponents of Abstract Expressionism.

Avant-garde: Artistic groups or approaches that are ahead of their time.

Barbizon School: A group of French painters who set an influential precedent by devoting themselves to 'plein-air' painting (s.v.) after 1840.

Baroque (from *barocco*, Port. '-irregular'): Style of art and architecture characterized by extreme dynamism and the dramatic use of space and light, practised between *c*. 1600 and *c*. 1750, initially in Rome and subsequently in a variety of forms and religious affiliations throughout Europe.

Bauhaus: School of art and design founded in Germany in 1919 by the architect Walter Gropius, whose aim was to unite all the arts under the primacy of architecture.

Biedermeier: Style of fine and decorative art in Germany and Austria from *c*. 1815 to 1848. In painting characterized by middle-class subjects and most notably represented by Carl Spitzweg.

Der Blaue Reiter (Ger. The Blue Rider): Title of an almanac containing theoretical essays on a variety of artistic topics, edited by Wassily Kandinsky and Franz Marc and published in 1910, and subsequently the name of a group of artists headed by Kandinsky and Marc who, influenced by Cubism (s.v.) and Orphism, rejected academic painting and Impressionism and attempted to express 'the spiritual in art' by semi-abstract means.

Die Brücke (Ger. The Bridge): Association of Expressionist artists that existed from 1905 to 1913. The work of the 'Brücke' artists features intense colours and a flat style with bold outlines and a starkness reminiscent of woodcut images.

Caravaggisti: Artists influenced by Caravaggio who adopted his bold chiaroscuro and the realistic treatment of Classical subjects.

Colour-Field painting: Type of all-over painting in Abstract Expressionism, notably in the 1960s, in which colour is applied in large areas with no distinct motifs in such a way as to suggest that it reaches beyond the confines of the picture plane. Important representatives include Barnett Newman and Mark Rothko.

Composition: Formal structure ordered according to certain basic principles, including the relationship of colour and form, symmetry and asymmetry, movement, rhythm etc.

Conceptual art: International art movement, initiated in the late 1960s, that declared intellectual processes to constitute a work of art in themselves, without being embodied in physical form.

Constructivism: Abstract art movement particularly influential in the 1920s and 1930s that attempted to create harmonious structures from purely non-representational, geometrical forms.

Cubism: Style of painting conceived by Pablo Picasso and Georges Braque *c*. 1907 in which objects are broken down into a series of shapes, often geometrical, in an attempt to depict them in their entirety rather than as they appear to the eye. A distinction is made between Analytic Cubism (until *c*. 1911) and Synthetic Cubism (1912 until the mid-1920s).

Dada: Art movement begun during the First World War that combated traditional artistic values by employing 'nonsensical' means of expression, including photomontage,

sound poems and other forms of 'anti-art'.

De Stijl: Dutch artists' group set up in 1917 by Piet Mondrian and Theo van Doesburg, whose abstract paintings, constructed from geometrical forms in pure colours, represent a variation of Constructivism.

Drip painting: Technique in which paint is dripped on canvas often laid on the floor. Mainly associated with Jackson Pollock.

Early Modernism: The avant-garde movements in the art of the first half of the twentieth century that, taking their cue from the work of Paul Cézanne, rejected traditional modes of expression, embracing abstraction and other innovatory means of expression.

Expressionism: Art movement in the first half of the twentieth century that stressed subjective experience. Characterized by highly expressive, non-naturalistic colours and forms employed in such a way as to combat any sense of three-dimensionality.

Fauvism, Fauves (Fr. 'wild beasts'): A loose association of French artists, formed around Henri Matisse in 1905, who rejected the Impressionist breakdown of colour in order to construct images from pure, unbroken colour that ignored naturalistic representation.

Fluxus: Loose international group of artists, musicians and writers who embraced random processes and staged interdisciplinary happenings (s.v.) from the 1960s to the late 1970s.

Fontainebleau, School of: Group of Italian, French and Flemish artists who, commissioned to decorate the royal château at Fontainebleau near Paris, developed a decorative, ornamental variant of Mannerism.

Futurism: Italian avant-garde art movement founded by the writer Filippo Tommaso Marinetti with the publication of the *Futurist Manifesto*. The anti-academic approach of the artists in the group embraced imagery celebrating modern technology and speed.

Genre painting: Art showing scenes from daily life. It ranked among the 'low' categories of painting in the academic hierarchy of artistic genres, and is generally marked by a high degree of realism. Divided into categories – images of peasant, middle-class and court life – it experienced a heyday in the

Netherlands in the seventeenth-century.

Happening: Type of art event practised chiefly in the 1960s, in which the work of art consists of activities that aim to involve viewers. The actions are improvised, unpredictable and impossible to reproduce.

Hard-Edge painting: Type of painting, chiefly abstract, in the 1960s and 1970s featuring clearly defined, often geometrical areas of flat colour. A variant of Colour-Field painting (s.v.).

History painting: Type of figure painting depicting subjects derived from history, mythology, religion and literature in a grand way, either idealized or naturalistic. Ranked highest among artistic genres in academic theory, followed by portrait painting and the 'low' genres of landscape (s.v.), genre (s.v.) and still life (s.v.).

Historicism: Revival of earlier styles, particularly in architecture and the decorative arts, to form new ones – for example, Neoclassicism (s.v.).

Icon: Image of a saint or other holy personages in the Byzantine Church and the Orthodox Churches of Greece and Russia, created for centuries in accordance with a strict formal idiom. Today the term is often used to signify a typical or classic example of something.

Impressionism: Movement in painting that emerged in France in the 1860s. The Impressionists aimed to capture fleeting visual 'impressions', chiefly by depicting atmospheric effects of light. Their preferred subjects included landscape and scenes of urban life.

Installation: One-off work of contemporary art conceived for and usually filling a particular space.

Jugendstil: German term for Art Nouveau (s.v.).

Kinetic art (from Gk. *kinesis*, 'movement'): Objects or paintings incorporating real or suggested movement.

Landscape painting: Paintings dominated by the depiction of the natural world. Originally forming backgrounds in other types of painting, landscape had become established as a pictorial genre in its own right by the late sixteenth century. The seventeenth century saw the emergence of 'ideal landscapes' (e.g., Claude Lorrain's idealized views) and 'heroic landscapes' (e.g., Nicolas

Poussin's symbolically charged images). Landscape painting reached its first peak of popularity in the Netherlands in the seventeenth century. The genre was revolutionized in the nineteenth century by plein-air painting (s.v.).

Mannerism: Term coined in the twentieth century to describe European art from c. 1515 to c. 1610, which is typified by bizarre effects of scale, lighting or perspective and elongated figures depicted in extreme poses. In the broader sense, Mannerism denotes a style that embraces exaggerated, distorted or artificial effects.

Minimal art: Flourishing in the 1960s and 1970s, a kind of abstract art marked by extreme simplicity of form and devoid of overt expressive content. Notable aspects are the repetition of basic – generally geometrical – structures and the eschewal of all manner of illusion, metaphor and symbolism.

Naïve art: Painting – and to a lesser extent sculpture – produced by untrained artists with a European cultural background. Free of academic tradition, naïve artists lend fantastical form to subjects taken from real life or the imagination, often in an awkward, childlike manner.

Naturalism: Artistic tendency prevalent throughout Europe in the second half of the nineteenth century in which artists attempted to render objects in terms of empirical observation rather than stylization.

Nazarenes: Group of idealistic German artists who in 1809–10 formed a 'brotherhood' on medieval lines in Vienna, subsequently moving to Rome. Their paintings were indebted stylistically to the work of Albrecht Dürer, Pietro Perugino and the young Raphael.

Neoclassicism: Flourishing from 1750 to 1840, a style of painting, sculpture and decoration based on the art and architecture of Classical Antiquity. It is characterized by a predilection for the linear and the symmetrical, and for flatness rather than plasticity.

Neue Sachlichkeit (Ger., New Objectivity): Movement in German painting in the 1920s and early 1930s that rejected the intense subjectivity of Expressionism in favour of 'objective' observation.. Characterized by meticulous detail, it is an emphatically representational style.

Neue Wilde (Ger., New Wild Ones): Group of Neo-Expressionist painters in Germany in the 1980s who employed an expressive, gestural style without regard to conventional notions of skill.

Nouveau réalisme (Fr. New Realism): Movement from 1960 onwards in which three-dimensional objects from everyday surroundings, usually mass-produced consumer goods, were incorporated into installations (s.v.) and environments.

Op art (abbrev. for 'Optical art'): Abstract art form that had its heyday in the 1960s. Op art engages with dynamic effects of colour and movement, stimulating the eye to perceive flat, multi-coloured patterns in terms of three-dimensional, vibrating structures.

Performance art: Action-based art form practised since the mid-1970s . Unlike happenings (s.v.), performance art is not improvised and does not involve audience participation.

Plein-air painting: Paintings produced in the open air, favoured by the Barbizon School (s.v.) and the Impressionists (s.v.).

Pointillism (from French point, 'dot'): A variant of Neo-Impressionism that juxtaposes small touches of pure colour such that the 'optical mixture' occurs in the eye of the beholder, not on the painter's palette.

Pop art: Movement flourishing primarily in America and Britain from the late1950s to the early 1970s that was based on the imagery of consumerism and popular culture, drawing on newspaper cuttings, comic strips, advertising and packaging. Its major exponents include Andy Warhol, Roy Lichtenstein and Allen Jones.

Postmodernism: Term taken from architecture for the prevailing artistic attitude since the early 1980s. It represents an attempt to modify and extend Modernism; unlike the tradition of Modernism (see 'Early Modernism), however, it rejects all ideologies and classical allegiances. Typified by stylistic quotation and individualistic artistic modes of expression.

Precisionism (also known as Cubist Realism): A movement in American painting – originating c. 1915 and experiencing its heyday in the inter-war years – in which objects were rendered realistically, but with an emphasis on their geometrical forms. A major development in American Modernism, it was inspired by Cubism (s.v.). Artists such as Charles Sheeler and Charles Demuth are most closely associated with the movement. Georgia O'Keeffe's paintings of urban scenes are also highly typical of this style. Dealing as it did with pure form more than with narrative or subject matter, Precisionism gradually evolved towards abstraction, eventually losing its importance.

Primitivism: Trend in the art of the twentieth century to turn to folk art or the art of Africa and Oceania, as well as to children's drawings, because they are more primal and 'unacademic', hence more 'authentic'.

Realism: In the broadest sense, a term signifying accurate, objective representation. At the same time, a movement in – chiefly French – art in the second half of the nineteenth century characterized by a rebellion against the idealistic tendencies of Romanticism in favour of unidealized scenes of modern life.

Regionalism: Regionalism refers to the work of a group of rural American artists, mostly from the Midwest, who came to prominence in the 1930s. Not being part of a coordinated movement, Regionalists often had an idiosyncratic style or approach. What they shared, along with other American Scene painters, was a humble, anti-modernist style and a fondness for depicting everyday life. Their rural conservatism put them at odds with the urban, leftist Social Realists, who flourished at the same time.

Renaissance (Fr. 'rebirth'): Classically inspired revival of European arts and letters, which began in Italy in the fourteenth century and exerted a profound influence on other parts of Europe.

Rococo (from French rocaille, 'shell-shaped ornaments'): Style of art and architecture in Europe from 1730 to 1770/80. The Rococo is predominantly a decorative style, which embraced lightness, elegance and playfulness, with a palette of light pinks, blues and greens.

Romanticism: Movement in the arts flourishing in the late eighteenth and early nineteenth centuries. Essentially a reaction against the rationalism and formality of Neoclassicism (s.v.), Romanticism is a deeply felt style that is at once individualistic and emotionally charged. It is characterized by atmospheric landscapes and a return to medieval legends and history. Artists closely associated with Romanticism include J. M. W. Turner, Caspar David Friedrich, John Constable and William Blake. In the United States, the late Romantic movement in painting was led by the Hudson River School, which produced dramatic landscapes.

Salon painting: By and large a pejorative term for painting executed in the academic style, which was practised towards the end of the nineteenth century and catered for bourgeois tastes.

Sezession: Name adopted by several groups of painters in Germany and Austria that broke away, or 'seceded', from the official academies. The first Sezession was founded in Munich in 1892; others followed some years later, in Vienna and Berlin.

Still life: Painting featuring inanimate objects, such as fruit, dead animals, flowers or everyday objects, often of a symbolic nature. Flourished in seventeenth-century Dutch painting, after having been considered a 'low' genre.

Suprematism: Russian abstract art movement, developed by Kasimir Malevich in the first two decades of the twentieth century, in which 'pure artistic feeling' was to be evoked solely by geometrical, abstract forms.

Surrealism: Movement in art and literature defined in 1924 in the first Surrealist manifesto written by André Breton. Its intention was to capture the irrational and the uncontrollable through associative thought processes and psychoanalytic explorations of the unconscious and dreams.

Symbolism: Movement in the second half of the nineteenth century that rejected the representation of visible reality in favour of the world of ideas, fantasies, visions and dreams.

Vanitas (Lat. 'vanity'): An allegorical still life (or part of a painting) that serves as a reminder of the inevitability of death, and the pointlessness of earthly ambitions and achievements. Common vanitas symbols include skulls, guttering candles, hourglasses and clocks, overturned vessels and flowers (which will soon fade). This type of painting became popular during the Baroque period, most notably in seventeenth-century Dutch painting.

Woodcut: Printing technique in which the image is cut into a wooden block. Used in the early years of the twentieth century by the Expressionists (s.v.).

Index

Photographic Credits

© Prestel Verlag, Munich · Berlin · London · New York, 2003
The Library of Congress Cataloguing-in-Publication data is available;
British Library Cataloguing-in-Publication Data: a catalogue record for this book is available from the British Library;
Die Deutsche Bibliothek holds a record of this publication in the Deutsche Nationalbibliografie; detailed bibliographical data can be found under:
http://dnb.ddb.de

Prestel books are available worldwide.
Please contact your nearest bookseller or one of the following
Prestel offices for information concerning your local distributor:

Prestel Verlag
Königinstrasse 9, 80539 Munich
Tel. +49 (89) 38 17 09-0; Fax +49 (89) 38 17 09-35

Prestel Publishing Ltd.
4 Bloomsbury Place, London WC1A 2QA
Tel. +44 (20) 7323-5004; Fax +44 (20) 7636-8004

Prestel Publishing
175 Fifth Avenue, Suite 402, New York, NY 10010
Tel. +1 (212) 995-2720; Fax +1 (212) 995-2733
www.prestel.com

Editor: Silke Körber / Delius Producing Berlin
Assistance: Hanno Deppner, Stephanie Esser
Indexing: Claudia Tscheuschner
Picture research: Katleen Krause

Translated from the German by Stephen Telfer, Edinburgh
Copy-edited by Michele Schons, Munich
Designed and typeset by Delius Producing Berlin
Originations by Bildpunkt, Berlin
Printed by Sellier Druck, Freising
Bound by Conzella, Pfarrkirchen

Printed in Germany on acid-free paper

ISBN 3-7913-2967-7